FOUL DEEDS AND SUSPICIOUS DEATHS IN GLASGOW

TRUE CRIME FROM WHARNCLIFFE

Foul Deeds and Suspicious Deaths Series

OTHER TRUE CRIME BOOKS FROM WHARNCLIFFE

Please contact us via any of the methods below for more information or a catalogue.

WHARNCLIFFE BOOKS

47 Church Street – Barnsley – South Yorkshire – S70 2AS
Tel: 01226 734555 – 734222 Fax: 01226 – 734438
E-mail: enquiries@pen-and-sword.co.uk
Website: www.wharncliffebooks.co.uk

Foul Deeds & Suspicious Deaths in
GLASGOW

PAUL HARRISON

First published in Great Britain in 2009 by
Wharncliffe Local History
an imprint of
Pen & Sword Books Ltd
47 Church Street
Barnsley
South Yorkshire
S70 2AS

Copyright © Paul Harrison 2009

ISBN 978 1 84563 083 6

Typeset in 11/13pt Plantin by
Mac Style, Beverley, East Yorkshire

Printed and bound in the UK by
the MPG Books Group

Pen & Sword Books Ltd incorporates the imprints of Pen & Sword
Aviation, Pen & Sword Maritime, Pen & Sword Military, Wharncliffe Local
History, Pen and Sword Select, Pen and Sword Military Classics and
Leo Cooper.

For a complete list of Pen & Sword titles please contact
PEN & SWORD BOOKS LIMITED
47 Church Street, Barnsley, South Yorkshire, S70 2AS, England
E-mail: enquiries@pen-and-sword.co.uk
Website: www.pen-and-sword.co.uk

Contents

Preface and Acknowledgements

My ancestral roots are in Scotland, in Edinburgh and Glasgow, two fair cities which hold many positive memories for me, particularly as a frequent childhood visitor, calling upon relatives and family friends and receiving the most hospitable of welcomes; the countless Hogmanay celebrations that seemed to go on for many days, weeks even. It is a place that always felt like home. Curious then, that this book should discuss memories, recollections, details and facts of a more unusual and macabre kind, indeed a most murderous kind.

I cannot quite remember what age I was when my grandfather, himself a police officer, first related the case details of 'Bible John' (Chapter 16) to me, certainly I was still in short trousers and not yet quite ready for secondary school education. Bible John terrified me, I expected to see him in every back street, every area of darkness, in cupboards and in the attic of our home. In my mind he was very much a portent of evil, something the stuff of nightmares. Almost forty years later, with at least fifteen of them spent researching the case, I remain curious about him.

As an ex-police officer who served throughout three decades I am nothing but supportive of the task facing the lads in blue, the Glasgow force in particular has an outstanding record of competently dealing with issues during times of extreme adversity. Therefore I want to thank those officers, back in the 1960s, 1970s and 1980s who rank amongst the best in the world.

My thanks go to Amanda Harrison, herself a True Crime enthusiast and historian. Without her support I would not be where I am today. I also want to mention Paula, Mark, Mia, Thomas, Morgan, Amber and Mercedes, each of whom has been a source of inspiration one way or another; but not forgetting the wonderful distractions that are Bingo and Angel.

Thanks too to the staff of the following newspapers for their support and the kind provision of illustrations for this work:

The Scottish Record Office
Glasgow Police Museum
The *Glasgow Times*
Glasgow Evening News
Daily Record
Scottish Daily Mail
The *Sunday Post*

The above have provided the background data and articles covering some of the crimes in this volume; and also have given permission to use many of the illustrations.

Thanks to Strathclyde, Lothian and Borders, and the Glasgow police forces respectively. Without them, none of this would have been possible; and my appreciation to the dozens of retired officers, too numerous to mention here, who recounted some of the anecdotes and finer details of criminal investigations. Sincere appreciation also goes to my publishers, especially to Rupert Harding for his support and belief in the subject and project. Finally, I want to thank the late Detective Inspector Joe Beattie, whose pride in the uniform, passion for the city, dedication and commitment to solving crime was a great help and inspiration, especially regarding the Bible John case. This book is dedicated to the memory of Joe Beattie.

CHAPTER 1

The Dawn of Doctor Frankenstein: Matthew Clydesdale

1818

If ever a case existed that displayed the absolute terror inflicted upon a ruthless and callous murderer then the file against Matthew Clydesdale is the one that draws conclusive evidence that the 'eye for an eye' rule does have an impact, and strikes fear into offenders found guilty in a court of law.

Matthew Clydesdale was an athletic and powerfully-built weaver, aged about thirty years, who lived in the village of Drumgalloch near Airdrie in Lanarkshire, then about fifteen miles from Glasgow. Arrogant and full of himself, there were few people locally who liked his bragging attitude and general approach towards the fairer sex. Indeed, rumours abounded that some time around the year 1815, Clydesdale had murdered a woman, yet had escaped detection. Always keen to show off and to get one over on another person, Clydesdale believed himself to be better than anyone at everything, and he would regularly win wagers with those who dared compete against him.

It was one such incident that led to murder early in the morning of 27 August 1818. The previous day had seen Matthew Clydesdale win a foot race against fellow weaver, William More, at Clarkston. With the winnings, Clydesdale had gone out celebrating with his brother, John, his friend James Rankine and his losing opponent, William More. The group merrily drank the night away in a pub at Clarkston Toll, where Clydesdale entertained his companions with some of his best singing. At around two the following morning, the landlord managed to turn out his noisy guests. James Rankine and John Clydesdale bid Matthew a goodnight and left him in the company of a tired William More who himself was keen to get home to his bed. Matthew Clydesdale would have none of it and demanded that More stay with him to celebrate.

The situation was rather delicate, as More had not envisaged spending so much time with the boastful Clydesdale. In an effort to get away from him for the night, he offered him a repeat of the foot race they had participated in less than twenty-four hours earlier. Clydesdale couldn't resist it and, although under the influence of alcohol, he was fully coherent and in charge of his senses. The route took the two men out of Clarkston, toward Drumgelloch. Soon after the race started, Clydesdale went off along a different route, no doubt believing it to be a shortcut and a course that would lead him to a second victory over More.

It wasn't long after he disappeared that William More heard a high pitched scream of 'Murder!' He stopped in his tracks, instinctively believing it to be the distressed cry of a woman. Recollections of the rumours that surrounded Matthew Clydesdale and the alleged murder he was supposed to have committed a few years earlier came flooding back to More. He elected to run to towards the area where the cry had emanated. Unbeknown to him, the high pitched cry had come from the voice of a fifteen-year-old boy, Alexander Love, who was walking to work for the morning shift at the Blackridge coal pit with his elderly grandfather, also called Alexander.

William More, whilst en route to the scene of the shout, heard, in the dark, the noise of a person groaning and clearly in distress. He stopped and found Mr Love senior laid by the side of the road. In the distance he heard someone cry out: 'That's a murdered man,' before running off and disappearing into the night in the direction of Matthew Clydesdale's home. He recognised the voice as being that of Matthew Clydesdale. Within seconds, More was joined at the scene by the victim's son, William Love who had been alerted of the situation by Alexander junior. The badly wounded man was carried home where he expired a few days later, his injuries coming as a result of the shocking and unprovoked attack upon him. Young Alexander Love claimed that he saw and knew the identity of his grandfather's attacker. It was Matthew Clydesdale.

The young boy stated that he and his grandfather had reached the junction of the main Glasgow to Edinburgh Road, which was about 200 yards from their home, when Clydesdale appeared and threatened them without any provocation. His grandfather had done nothing wrong, when suddenly Clydesdale began to beat him with a stick that he had picked up from the floor. In his panic, the young boy had fled back to his home for help. Screaming murder, he dropped a coal pick that he had been carrying. Turning round to look back at what was happening to his grandfather as he ran, he saw Clydesdale grab the pick, raise it above his head and bring it down on the old man who had fallen to the ground.

Elsewhere, Matthew Clydesdale arrived home to find his brother, John and James Rankine, already there and waiting for him. On entering the house, the family cat gleefully ran up to welcome him. Clydesdale wanted no attention, so picked up the pet and threw it to the stone floor with some force. The poor creature was clearly in agony and suffering. Not content with this, Clydesdale again picked it up and threw it into the fire, telling those who witnessed this barbaric act of cruelty that it would prevent the cat from suffering further. Another person at the house, James Fairley, was later to recall the incident and also how dishevelled and on edge Clydesdale was when he got home. He had commented that it looked as though he (Clydesdale) had been in a fight. He noticed a wound to his knee and asked how it had been sustained. The ever arrogant Clydesdale claimed that he had been attacked on the road by 'two tinkers', adding: 'The man who wounded my knee will never do it again.' Fairley, recognised by the tone and purpose in Clydesdale's voice that he meant that he had killed the man. Despite this, not one of the group took it upon themselves to question him further or to report the matter to the magistrates.

Later that same day, the Love family received the expected and requested visit from the local magistrates. It was clear that the wounded Alexander Love was in the throes of death, he was unable to put together a sentence and drifted in and out of consciousness.

Young Alexander was the perfect witness, he provided every detail and named the attacker. Within hours, Matthew Clydesdale was arrested and taken into custody, where, a few days later, he was formally charged with the wilful murder of Alexander Love. The trial took place at Glasgow and was, for the best part, without any incident. It was reported that Clydesdale had viciously struck the seventy-year-old man four times with the coal pick, three times on his back and once to his head, smashing his skull and causing irreparable damage. Furthermore, he had also beaten him with a heavy stick, knocking him to the ground where he reigned kicks and further blows on the prostrate body that offered little resistance and that now lay beneath him. On hearing the evidence there was little in the way of compassion shown for the accused. The trial judge, Lord Gillies, in his summing up left no one in any doubt that he expected a verdict of guilty to be returned by the jury. His request did not go unheeded and so Matthew Clydesdale was found guilty of the murder of Alexander Love. The judge pronounced that Clydesdale was to hang in Glasgow on Wednesday 4 November 1818. He further added that the man, during his period of incarceration, should be fed only bread and water. After the execution, his body would be cut down and publicly dissected and anatomised. This addition caused the guilty man to recoil in horror, the thought of such experiences clearly affecting him.

In prison, Clydesdale reacted very badly and was terrified by the thought of the public dissection. He attempted to escape by cutting through bars on a cell window but was foiled in his efforts to do so. He also claimed to be tormented and haunted, having several visitations from the ghost of his victim, in his prison cell. Scant punishment for a senseless crime. Later, two days before his execution, he was unofficially granted a bottle of porter by the prison manager, John McGregor. The following morning, prison warders found Clydesdale laying in his cell, losing copious amounts of blood. He had deliberately smashed the bottle and used it to try to commit suicide in an attempt to ensure that he was dead when taken to for dissection. His wounds were patched up and he finally took the walk to the gallows in the afternoon of the allotted date, along with Simon

Ross who was a housebreaker and habitual offender, who had tried the courts patience once too often it seems.

The gallows had been erected in front of the new High Court building which had originally been opened in 1814. The expert executioner, Tammas Young, managed the first execution for murder in a decade in the city of Glasgow. As a result, a double hanging was something of a public spectacle and it is said that several thousand people packed into Jail Square which stood at the foot of Saltmarket, to witness the event. On the gallows, Clydesdale became remorseful and was in constant prayer, taking to his knees and begging forgiveness and mercy, too little, too late. Both men were efficiently dispatched from this earth, though it is said that Ross appeared to suffer at the end of the hangman's rope more than Clydesdale, twitching a jumping for several minutes before giving in to a permanent sleep.

Within an hour, both hanged men were officially pronounced dead. Clydesdale was cut down and his body placed in an open cart. Crowds booed and hissed at the corpse which was transported and escorted by armed guard along the Saltmarket through Trongate and along the High Street before finally arriving at Glasgow University.

For those who wished to further satiate their sanguinary desires, the public dissection wasn't about to be a run of the mill one, this was scientific experimentation at its wildest, 'galvanisation'. A few months earlier, author Mary Shelley had published her most famous novel, *Frankenstein*. This was

Galvanisation of killer Matthew Clydesdale.

Mary Shelley, author of Frankenstein.

regarded as a far fetched tale of resurrectionists or body snatchers; about a mad doctor whose experiments with dead bodies and how he used electricity to create a monster who consisted of many different parts from different dead owners, including criminals. Electrical energy was used to reinvigorate life into the creature.

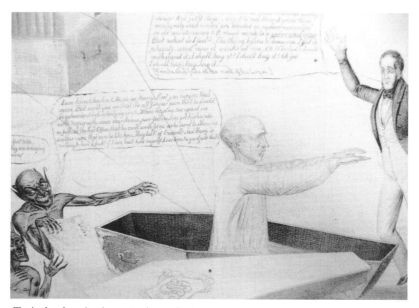

Typical galvanisation experiment in progress.

The term galvanisation is derived from the work of Professor Luigi Galvani, who in 1780 began a series of experiments running electricity through the bodies of dead frogs. He observed that the frogs' limbs twitched, as though in life. He harboured a scientific belief that dead human beings could be resuscitated by use of managed electrical force. His nephew, Giovanni Aldini, famously toured Europe performing to paying professional and public audiences, demonstrating the electrification of human and animal corpses. This sinister show evoked much emotional fright and horror amongst those who gathered to watch it, arousing anger, terror and intrigue wherever it was performed, thus assuring greater audiences at the following venue. Later, in 1803 at the Royal College of Surgeons, Aldini carried out a similar experiment on a hanged man, George Forster. Once again a large medical and general audience had gathered as Aldini, who now had his show off to a fine art, performed brilliantly. First, he took a pair of conducting rods that were crudely attached to a powerful battery. Then, systematically, he applied the rods to numerous parts of Forster's corpse. It is said that when the rods touched Forster's mouth and ears his jaw began to shake and quiver with the adjoining muscles becoming horribly contorted. At one point the left eye lifted giving the impression that he had opened his eye and was looking at Aldini. On another occasion a rod was inserted in Forster's rectum, causing the entire corpse to convulse and twitch. The actions became so increased that it provided a false appearance of re-animation, many of those present fled in terror while others simply vomited at the horror of it all. It was too much for one poor soul who passed out on the floor. The press of the day had a field day, recounting in detail the horrors on show, claiming that spectators genuinely believed that the body was about to come to life. Aldini himself was rather more conservative about these experiments, claiming that galvanisation exerted a considerable power over the nervous and muscular systems of the body, adding that nothing similar could currently be done with the heart but experimentation should continue. These they did, hence the modern day defibrillator.

Dr Ure who experimented on corpse of Clydesdale.

The body of Matthew Clydesdale was delivered to Dr Andrew Ure and Professor James Jeffrey, both of whom were great students and believers in Galvini and subsequently Aldini's work. Andrew Ure in particular was keen to extend Aldini's experimentations, using his own techniques. In the apartment that had been structured to replicate an operating theatre, a battery was prepared and charged with dilute nitric and sulphuric acids in order to provide the electricity that would allow the gathered throng to be entertained.

Clydesdale was stripped naked and laid out on the slab. The two doctors then made numerous incisions into the skin, and many of the public audience were shocked that Clydesdale did not bleed. Eventually, the corpse was ready to accept the electrical current. The rods were attached to the battery and the show, for this was no medical experiment, began. First, Ure inserted the electric rods into the incisions that had been made a short time earlier. There was instant response. As the current began to flow through the body, movement began. According to reports of the time, an application of a rod to the heel caused the leg to bend and then kick out with such violence that it very nearly overturned one of the unsuspecting assistants. The audience gasped in shock, causing the assistants to at once take hold of the limb and to try to prevent it from further movement and causing injury to an innocent party. A connection to the left phrenic nerve and the

Medical College where galvanisation experiments took place [building on left of illustration].

diaphragm caused a near perfect reproduction of breathing. The experiments continued: one rod was attached to the supra-orbital nerve of the forehead and another to the heel; and these were linked together resulting in most extraordinary grimaces and expressions upon the face of the corpse. The *Glasgow Times* newspaper recorded: 'Rage, horror, despair, anguish, and ghastly smiles, united their hideous expression in the murderer's face. At this period several of the spectators were forced to leave the apartment from terror or sickness...' Those who were brave enough to witness the entire show were petrified as a final rod was applied to the tip of an index finger. The digit rose up and extended, giving the appearance that it was pointing at individual spectators, many of whom believed that he (Matthew Clydesdale) had come back to life.

According to legend, the cadaver experiment had by this stage got out of hand and could only be stopped by Andrew Ure physically slitting the throat of the dead murderer. Once done, the corpse fell limp. The fact that the body did not have a beating heart and therefore had no blood coursing through its veins, hence severing the carotid artery would have had no physical effect on the corpse, was ignored by subsequent recorders of this same experiment. The reality was still dramatic, yet much more controlled, the muscles and nerves within the corpse continuing to respond to powerful electrical current.

In another story, Professor Jeffrey takes out a lancet and plunges it into the bewildered corpse's jugular vein. This caused it drop to the floor in a not dissimilar fashion to a slaughtered animal. It is gripping stuff yet definitely more akin to a horror film.

Andrew Ure himself was to later record an account of such procedures and makes a somewhat sensational passing mention that the placing of two moistened brass knobs on the skin, one over the phrenic nerve and the other over the diaphragm, and both attached to a battery, might be effective in restoring life to a dead individual.

Whatever the horrors were of the entire operation, it provided a fitting and ignominious end to the life of a vicious murderer who may well have been a double killer.

The public circus surrounding the public dissection had nothing but ill effects on entire communities, whose members spoke of its horrors in front of young children and thus perpetuated the legend of Frankenstein. There was also consideration given to how others seemed to make financial benefit from it, selling broadsheets and reporting on its gory detail in the press, increasing newspaper sales. This all caused the judiciary to rethink about how or when or why they should making such orders after an execution. Ultimately this was the last dissection order made by the circuit judges at Glasgow.

The crime committed by Matthew Clydesdale is one that will be remembered for different reasons, none of which involve him with dignity in life or death. For many years after it is said that the story of Matthew Clydesdale's suffering and torment was recalled in pubs and taverns throughout Scotland. Everything from his being haunted by his victim's ghost right through to his failure to commit suicide served as a warning that other, higher authorities were influencing the anguish he endured. It served as a grim warning to other potential killers.

CHAPTER 2

Ill Repute – Ill Fortune: William Divan

1824

estling on the south side of the River Clyde sits the Gorbals which has medieval origins. For a time it was widely regarded as Glasgow's leper colony. It is said that the Gorbals is so named as a result of those living in the colony, the residents of which were seemingly forced to ring a bell when they crossed the Clyde to enter the city. The bell was known as the Gorey Bell, hence the name Gorbals. The district increased in population over the years, and by the turn of the nineteenth century could boast a

Typical Gorbals scene of the last century.

population of around 5000. Essentially, it was little more than a cluster of seventeenth century thatched roofed buildings, often referred to as Gorbals Cross. However, it deteriorated as Irish immigrants poured into the area. With insufficent properties available and many of the older dwellings now in decay, buildings were restructured into single room accommodation, providing sanctuary for more people. As the overcrowding commenced, so did the general standard of hygiene and cleanliness of the district. It was generally described as a festering slum land, a breeding ground of filth and squalor. One unnamed local writer recorded his objections and sadness to the environment, saying:

> *We are really grieved to part with some of these old landmarks of the city, and we cannot help urging the proprietors of such houses as exist to pay some little attention to them, and above all to prevent them falling prey to the hordes of Irish immigrants who have a fancy to burrow in these ancient spots.*

Gorbals parish church c. eighteenth century.

The Main Street was extremely narrow in parts with scarcely a semblance of pavement. It was the epicentre of all activity, not only for trade, but as the main thoroughfare between the north and south. The one notable building was the mansion house of the Elphinstone family, standing on the corner of Main Street and Rutherglen Loan. This property towards the close of eighteenth century was turned into the police office, later becoming a public house. Running off the west side of the Main Street was Kirk Street, also Malta Street, known as Paisley Loan. It was in this street in 1824, that a callous and gruesome murder took place, a crime that left three innocent young children as orphans.

Irish born Mary Jamieson lived in Paisley Loan with William Divan. Mary was a woman of extremely good character and reputation. Her neighbours thought and spoke highly of her and how she would always do a good turn for them if asked by any of them. She would also listen to their problems and help out if she could. She was of a kindly disposition and went about her business with a smile etched upon her face. To anyone who didn't know her, she was a happy and content woman who managed her domestic matters, a husband and three children; and food bill payments in a proper and sensible manner. Her children were the most important things in her life. Beneath this facade her domestic life was miserable, her forty-seven-year old husband, William, was anything but kind or generous towards her.

He originated from Donegal in Ireland but had lived in Scotland for over thirty years, mostly within the Gorbals. A former weaver, he had dipped in and out of honest work as and when he needed to, much preferring to spend his time in an alcoholic stupor, committing crime in order to sustain his drinking habits. Rarely did he provide for his family, that was Mary's role. In times of desperation, Divan would help his wife sell fish on the streets, pocketing his earning and spending them the same day or night, caring little as to how or what his children would eat. Neighbours would speak of how violent he was towards his wife, never thinking twice about giving her a slap in the street if he didn't get his own way. One can only feel sympathy for his poor unfortunate wife who was treated like a slave.

On the morning of Tuesday 6 April 1824, Mary popped into a neighbour's home and asked to borrow a razor. William required a shave and saw it as Mary's job. She took the cut-throat and returned to her own rooms. At around two o'clock in the afternoon neighbours saw Mary's children returning to their home after a morning at the cotton mill, wanting food. Suddenly, the Paisley Loan area was filled with terrified screams and whooping shrieks of horror, coming from the mouths of children. It was clear to all those who heard the sound that it was not the sound of innocent play. Several people rushed to find the source of the noise and entered Mary Jamieson's home. There, her children were found, ashen faced and trembling, sobbing uncontrollably. They screamed out that their mother was dead. Moving into the bedroom, the neighbours cast their eyes on a morbid scene that would live with them forever more. There laid upon the bed was the body of Mary Jamieson, dressed, but her clothes saturated in her own blood.

Blood was spattered up the walls and great pools of it covered the wooden floor. Footprints to and from the bedside were clear for all to see. The children's prints were obvious, yet there was an adult set too, leading from the room. Closer inspection revealed that Mary's throat had been sliced open from ear to ear, crimson red blood still dripping from the gaping gash. Many of those who witnessed the carnage ran out into the street and were violently sick. Why would anyone want to do such a thing to a lovely woman like Mary?

The police were fetched from the nearby police station and soon found, laying on the chimney breast, a cut-throat razor, the blade and handle of which was covered in congealed blood. This was clearly the murder weapon. It was formally identified as being the one loaned to Mary that morning in order that she could shave her husband. Beneath the metal-framed bed lay a bundle of Mary's clothes. When these were recovered it was clear that they must have been worn by the woman during the frenzied attack. The clothes that her corpse had been dressed and found in had been placed upon her *after* she was dead. The amount of blood on these was not conducive to the amount that covered the bed, floor and walls, meaning the killer must have carried out this curious task. Even more strange was the fact that within Mary's purse was a small amount of money, thus proving that plunder had not been the motive of the crime.

Within minutes all the talk was about William Divan, the dead woman's husband, and how he was violent and knocked poor Mary about. He had been heard to threaten her in the past, saying that he would slit her throat if she did not give him money for drink and gambling. The police had a wanted person straight away and soon had him in custody. Divan denied all allegations made against him, but no one believed his protestations. He was charged with the murder of his wife and was tried at Edinburgh, on 14 June 1824, where, before judge and jury he was unanimously found guilty of murder. Throughout the proceedings, Divan denied the deed but few doubted his guilt. It is something of a sad indictment that we shall never truly know the motive behind the murder of Mary Jamieson. Speculation allows us to ponder whether it was yet another heated disagreement surrounding money that William Divan wanted and needed, and Mary's resolute defiance that the needs of children came first.

The verdict of the court was pronounced against him, and the Lord Justice clerk addressed him accordingly: 'Your days are numbered, you have cruelly bereft your wife of life, a wife who you ought to have protected and cherished. You stand this day at the bar another awful example that murder will not hide.'

In somewhat dramatic style the clerk then beseeched him to humble himself before God, whose laws he had so most grievously offended – mercy he had none, and none he could expect on earth, but may God have mercy upon his immortal soul. The seriousness of the situation caused William Divan to drop to his knees and sob. It was said that in the presence of the God before whom he was soon to appear, he solemnly protested his innocence of the crime for which he was to suffer. It was an act that fooled no one, clearly the man was terrified of the fate that awaited him. The broadsheet extracts of Divan's actions in court make compelling reading: 'Such an appeal as this, made by a person on the brink of eternity, and

Execution.

Account of the Execution and Behaviour on the Scaffold and since his Sentence, of WILLM. DIVAN, who suffered at Glasgow on Wednesday the 21st July, 1824, for the Murder of his own Wife, Mary Jamieson, in Paisley Loan, Gorbals, on the 6th day of April last, by cutting her throat, and his body given for dissection.

Glasgow, 21st July, 1824.—This day, the above unfortunate man forfeited his life for the murder of Mary Jamieson, his wife, in Paisley Loan, Gorbals, on the 6th day of April last. The woman was found dead by two of her own children, with her throat cut, when they came home to their dinner, who then gave the alarm, and the Police soon arrived and searched the house, but found nothing missing, so that plunder was not the object; neither could it be from the ill will of any of her neighbours, as she lived on the most friendly terms with them, and was loved by all who knew her, for her kindly disposition, and for the careful manner with which she managed her domestic concerns, especially her children. We fear very (though the prisoner has all along denied the commission of the horrid deed) that he was really the guilty person. There is not an individual who read the trial, but will be as fully convinced as the Judges and Jury of the fairness of the verdict, which was pronounced against him, and on the issue of which being made known to the prisoner, and after the Lord Justice Clerk had addressed him in these words; ("his days were numbered; he had cruelly bereft his wife of life, whom he ought to have protected and cherished; you stand this day at the bar another awful example that "murder will not hide;" he then beseeched him to humble himself before God, whose laws he had so most grievously offended—mercy he had none, and none he could expect on earth, but may God have mercy upon his immortal soul;)" even after this solemn address, and all the advantages of a fair trial, conducted by upright Judges and a respectable jury, who would undoubtedly look to the side of mercy, were the least doubt remaining of his guilt, the prisoner on his bended knees, and in the presence of that God before whom he was soon to appear, solemnly protests his innocence of the crime for which he is to suffer.— Such an appeal as this, made by a person on the brink of eternity, and knowing himself to be actually guilty, fills us with horror, and makes us shudder at the idea of a man going to the just tribunal of God with a lie in his right hand.

Since his condemnation he has been assisted in his devotional exercises by two of the Ministers of the Church of Rome, the Rev. Messrs. Scott and Murdoch of Glasgow, who visited him frequently, and paid every attention to his comfort and edification. He was also attended by them in his cell on the day of execution, (the difference in the forms of worship rendering the usual solemnities in the Hall unnecessary), and from that to the scaffold, which he ascended in a very becoming manner, and after spending a few moments on the fatal drop in communion with his conscience and his God, he gave the signs, and after a few convulsive pangs he was ushered into that state where the secrets of the heart are naked and open to Him with whom he has to do.—After being suspended for about 35 minutes, his body was cut down, and conveyed in a coffin, and under a military escort, to Dr. Jeffray, Professor of Anatomy in Glasgow, to be publicly dissected.—He was decently dressed, and was about 47 years of age.—He originally belonged to the county of Donegal, Ireland, but has been in this country upwards of 30 years, a number of which he has spent in the Gorbals of Glasgow, and resided at the time of committing the deed in Paisley Loan. He was some time a weaver, but latterly sold fish along with his wife upon the streets. She also belonged to Ireland. By this horrid business, three children have been deprived of their parents, an awful lesson to every person to beware of hasty passion, bad company, and every thing that would, in any way, lead them from the paths of honest industry, or that would tempt them to gratify their desires at the expense of the life of a fellow creature, and especially of any one whom they are bound by the most endearing ties to protect and watch over.—He was tried at Edinburgh, on the 15th June; was sent back here on the 21st of the same, to undergo the sentence passed upon him, which was put in force this day, the 21st July, 1824.

W. Carse, Printer, Glasgow.

knowing himself to be actually guilty, fills us with horror, and makes us shudder at the idea of a man going to the just tribunal of God with a lie in his right hand.'

William Divan was sent back to Glasgow on 21 July 1824, to serve the sentence that had been passed upon him. Broadsheet extracts denote the days leading up to his execution by William Calcraft: 'Since his condemnation he has been assisted in his devotional exercises by two of the Ministers of the Church of Rome, the Rev. Messrs. Scott and Murdoch of Glasgow, who visited him frequently, and paid every attention to his comfort and edification. He was also attended by them in his cell on the day of execution (the difference in the forms of worship rendering the usual solemnities in the hats unnecessary). He ascended the scaffold in a very becoming manner and, after spending a few moments on the fatal drop in commission with his conscience and his God, he gave the signal, and after a few convulsive pangs was ushered into that state where the secrets of the heart are naked and open to him with whom he has to do.'

The body of William Divan was left suspended above the pit for around thirty-five minutes, until a period of muscle twitching and murmuring (through the expulsion of body gases) ceased. It then hung limp like the carcass of a dead pig in a butcher's shop. Eventually it was cut down from the rope. The hangman, as was the occasional custom, was given the opportunity to take possession of the deceased's clothing, available to sell on to the highest bidder as morbid souvenirs of the event. The body was then conveyed in a makeshift wooden coffin and taken under military escort to Dr James Jeffrey, Professor of Anatomy at Glasgow University in order that it could be publicly dissected by him for experimental purposes.

Many of the press reports of the day refer to the couple's surname as being Devon as opposed to Divan. The majority of the records viewed indicate the latter as being the correct name, albeit an Irish brogue would provide a name sounding remarkably similar. The fact that the murder victim, Mary Jamieson, preferred to use this as her surname indicates the lack of affection between the couple. One can only feel sadness that such a genuine woman should meet her end in such a despicable manner, when it seems clear that her intent was to simply satiate her husbands needs by giving him the shave he demanded. It should be added that throughout the giving of evidence at the trial, no strangers or suspicious circumstances came to light, and the police could find no one with any grudge or grievance to hold against the unfortunate victim. William Divan was the only suspect and the only one who ever spoke badly of Mary Jamieson. There remains no doubt as to his guilt.

Chapter 3

Roasted: George Duffy

1832

Glasgow in the 1830s had a population of over 200,000, especially concentrated in the congested and busy inner city area. The pressure of urban saturation and overcrowding caused much in the way of segregation as the East End became inhabited by working class folk, the majority of whom were employed in the production of textiles. Conversely, the West End became inhabited mostly by the middle classes. The constant fluidity and rise in the population of the city put a continual strain on the supply of basic essentials of food and water. In some areas the poor found it increasingly difficult to find adequate supplies of either and as poverty and all its associated illnesses and ailments took hold, crime increased and law and order decreased as people desperately resorted to anything to survive. The side effects of the industrial upturn were obvious for all to see, with greatly polluted rivers and streams and the air quality heavily affected by the onset of steam power.

The drinking culture of Glasgow was deemed responsible for the anti-social behaviour exhibited by many of the young. There were many places where alcohol was readily available and cheap to purchase no matter what age you were. Every now and then occasions such as the Glasgow Fair or Hogmanay even, meant that drink was inextricably linked to life in Glasgow. Although women did drink, many of the clubs, taverns and 'tippling houses' were frequented and exclusively available only to men. Women at this time tended to be caught up in the world of community activity and charitable organisations. For many, the church became their focus. Early nineteenth-century Glasgow was far from being a socially balanced city; it was however a working class a community with loyalty far beyond the understanding of the upper classes. Many of these folk were the salt of the earth and would do anything for a neighbour or a friend.

Drygate Street in Glasgow was one of the oldest thoroughfares in the city in 1832, where George Duffy and his family resided. George was a forty-five-year-old Irish Catholic originally from Green Castle in Ireland. Like so many immigrants he had come to Glasgow seeking a new life and his fortune. He was was renowned for his heavy drinking and brutish and abusive behaviour towards his wife, Helen Duffy nee Broadly. Helen was a tiny lady, small framed and barely five feet tall. She was known to have a friendly and mild disposition. George, it would seem, saw Helen as a threat to his less than admirable habits and would often be heard to thrash her in their home when things didn't go his way.

Helen was an industrious woman and worked hard cleaning houses and at any other work she could find locally. Although George also worked cleaning and emptying dungsteads (effluent tanks), it was known that Helen shared her money with George willingly and was generous to him. George frittered away most of the cash he earned on drink and made little in the way of positive contribution to the household. We may ask ourselves why Helen stayed with George as he was more than frequently abusive to her, mentally, emotionally and physically. Yet at that time a woman with a child had very few choices available to her, the only viable option was to stay if she found herself in a violent relationship, it put a roof over her and the families head and food on the table and that was all that was important.

Alexander Godan and his wife had lodged in the same house as the Duffy's for around eight months and were frequent witnesses to George's behaviour towards Helen, indeed on several occasions it had been necessary for Alexander to intervene to prevent George from severely hurting her. This generally resulted in the bullying husband backing down and doing a lot of shouting. It wasn't a pleasant environment for anyone to live in. Poor Helen took the brunt of every failing in George Duffy's miserable life.

On 14 May 1832, a stranger, a woman, came to the house. Helen spoke with the woman who said she needed to speak with Mr Duffy, in relation to an outstanding debt. Helen went into an instant panic, never before had she had the debt collectors round at her door. Money that she had given George to pay the rent had been spent on drink. Helen did her best to explain how the debt had occurred. However, the woman was insistent that she speak with George as soon as possible. As George was not at home, both Helen and the woman went in search of him. They found him in a pub, where George was confronted by the debt collector and publicly shamed when she asked him for the rent money he had wasted.

Later that same day, Alexander Godan returned to the rooms in the Duffy household that he loosely referred to as his home. He was unaware of the debt problem and the resultant discontent that would arouse within the household. On climbing the stairs, he heard passive whimpering and painful moaning coming from the Duffy bedroom. Concerned, he knocked and entered the room to find Helen in bed, clearly suffering and with bruises on her face. From the way he could hear her groaning in pain he realised that she was physically struggling. George was also present and instead of being comforting towards his wife, he paced up and down and continued to shout abuse at her. Every so often he demanded that she 'get out of the bed'. The unfortunate woman laboured in her attempts to rise from the bed and could hardly move a muscle. It was clear that in her current state it was impossible for her to do as George ordered. Alexander had seen enough, he angrily took George to task for his behaviour and told him to treat his wife with greater consideration and care. When all was quiet, he left the room and returned to his wife and quarters, stating that the sooner they got out and away of the Duffy house the better it would be for all concerned. Everyone that is, except Helen who would undoubtedly suffer more without Alexander Godan's interventions.

All that evening and through into the night, Helen could be heard moaning and crying in agony. Alexander and his wife were aware of a strange burning odour that filled the air. It was something they could not identify and was believed to be coming from the surrounding streets outside. Every so often George could be heard shouting at his wife, making no effort to comfort or support her. In one fit of rage he blurted out a frightening comment that caused both of the Godans to shiver in horror at the very thought of the threat. George told Helen that he wished he could bury her the next day.

The following morning at five o'clock, Alexander Godan was getting ready to leave for his work as a weaver. He called in to check on the state of Helen Duffy and on seeing that she was still in much pain, he went to fetch a glass of water, which she gratefully accepted and tried to drink. He noticed that she was struggling to move and was sweating profusely. It was clear that George Duffy had not cared for his wife at all during the night despite her obvious pain. He was sat, sleeping in a nearby chair, totally oblivious as to Alexander Godan's presence in the room.

Later that morning, at around 9.00 am, Alexander Godan returned home for his breakfast. All was quiet so he did not disturb Helen Duffy and returned to his work. At sometime around 2.00 pm he returned once more, this time for his lunch. On entering the house he was surprised to see Helen Duffy sitting by the fireside wearing just her shift and with her petticoat around her shoulders. She looked dreadful and instantly asked Alexander if he could get her to the infirmary as she was in terrible pain. She reiterated that George, her own husband, would not help her. Little could have prepared Alexander for what was next about to happen. Helen showed him the injuries she had sustained from her husband the previous evening. She was covered in burns. Not minor or superficial ones but serious amounts of flesh had suffered traumatic injury. There was deep raw flesh burns on her thighs and stomach and further, more severe burns on her buttocks and back. It was incredible the poor woman was still alive. Helen then told Alexander how the burns had been administered. It was chilling and ghoulish. George had given her yet another beating, not satisfied with this he then cut up her clothes and forcefully lifted her, dropping her onto the roaring and red hot open fire where he held her down in order that she could not escape the flames. He turned her over onto her front for a few seconds then over again onto her back, punching and hitting her lower body all the time. Eventually, he was overcome by the heat and had let her go, dropping her to the floor, still shouting at her as she lay there, her body literally smoking. Eventually, she had managed to get into bed.

Alexander was mortified by what he heard and horrified by the injuries he saw on Helen's body. He at once went to see George, who was lying in bed. He asked Duffy what he had done to Helen, to which George insensitively and flippantly replied: 'She had taken a half-crown from his pocket and it was rent day.' The comment was made as though to justify his treatment of his wife. He told George Duffy: 'You have settled her now, she's terribly burnt, she's roasted.' At no time did George deny burning Helen, but he did not admit to it either, and despite everything he still refused to help his wife in any way.

Alexander said that he had to return to his work, but he gave George an ultimatum before he left, saying that if he did not get Helen some help within the hour then he would be forced to inform the police of the situation. Eventually Helen did get to the infirmary but she was understandably extremely weak from her injuries and there was very little hope of her recovering. On 9 June, a full three weeks after her injuries were so cruelly inflicted, Helen died. Alexander's statement to the court was confirmed by his wife, Dr Stirling, the nurse, clerk and the surgeon of the Infirmary and many other witnesses besides.

George was arrested and further damning evidence was heard at his trial. Alexander gave evidence at George Duffy's trial that Helen was always covered in bruises and marks from the beatings she suffered at her husband's hands and he had heard Duffy threaten to 'burn' his wife.

It didn't take the jury long to unanimously find him guilty of the horrific crime. The judge, Lord Justice Clerk, is quoted as saying: 'This is the most atrocious case of brutal cruelty and severe barbarity.' He sentenced George Duffy to be executed by hanging on 7 November 1832 between the times of two and four o'clock and that thereafter his body would be buried with the confine of the precincts of the jail.

EXECUTION.

The Behaviour, Execution, and Life and Transactions of GEORGE DUFFY, who suffered at Glasgow on the 7th Nov. 1832, for the cruel and brutal Murder of his own Wife, in Drygate Street, in May last.

GLASGOW, 7th Nov. 1832.

This day, the above unfortunate individual suffered in front of the Jail here. The following is the substance of the way and manner in which he committed this horrid and brutal deed :—

George Duffy was indicted for the murder of Helen Broady, or Duffy, his wife, having violently seized her person, and by force carried her to and threw her upon the fire, and held her thereon, or close thereto, whereby she was so severely burnt in the back, belly, legs, and other parts of the body, as to linger from 14th May to 9th June, when she died—he having for several months previous used her with great cruelty.

Alexr Godin, weaver, deponed, that he and his wife lodged for eight months previous to May last, in the same house with [...] and his wife, who occupied the kitchen, while he occupied the room, which entered through the kitchen; had full opportunity of knowing on what terms Duffy and his wife lived; he was very violent in his temper, especially to her; has seen him thrash her, and was twice obliged to interfere to save her; she was seldom without marks of violence upon her body; Duffy was seldom sober; treated her of him being once sober for three days together. Mrs Duffy took a dram sometimes; saw her only once tipsy; her temper was easy; she did not provoke her husband—during the three days that I saw him so [...], he used his wife very harshly—saw him on two occasions knock her down—he [...] her to the floor. One day she had gone out with another person, and on her return Duffy took her to account, and said he would burn her. She was industrious, and had to work for herself and did every thing for her husband besides. He did all his earnings commonly—she washed cleaned houses, and any thing for industry, and [...] it with her husband. She was a little neat woman, about five feet high. He was asked if he recollected any thing particular happening on 14th May? Another woman came to ask for some money from Duffy, and his wife and this woman went to seek him. Witness came home about nine o'clock; as he came through the kitchen, Mrs D. was in bed; heard her husband say to her, ' you come out of that, or I'd hardly you to ——.'— Thought it is presence a right step him from worse, as it had once at before, and went into the kitchen to light his pipe and draw himself into conversation. Deceased moaned much as in distress, and said, in all probability, she would not see another day. Duffy said, it was to God I had you to bury to-morrow. She continued to moan the whole night; perceived an uncommon smell through that night, for which he could not account; it was a burnt-like smell—went to work next morning at five—gave deceased a drink of water, at her request, as he passed out—saw her in bed when he returned at nine to breakfast—and at two saw her on a seat by the fire with her shift on, and petticoat loose on her shoulders.— She called me, and said Sanders, will you be so good as go and make application to get me into the Infirmary? I asked her, what's wrong now? She said, my pain is so sore—and said she must show me her body. She [...] up her shift and showed her body; it was in a shocking state; the skin of the thighs and lower part of the body was off and all raw flesh, whether turned round and showed me her back; her hips and posterior was in the same state. I asked her how this had happened? She said George had given

her a beating—had torn up her clothes, and put her on the fire. George was in bed; went and pushed him to waken him, and said what's this you have done—you have settled her now—she's terribly burnt—she's roasted ? He said, swearing, she's not half roasted; she has taken a half crown from my pocket, and this is the rent day. She said, now God will reward you, George. I asked him to get a Doctor, and have her wounds dressed. He said he had no money; asked him to get some ointment and dress it himself, but he did not. He never denied roasting her. I went to work, and told him, that if he did not have her dressed before an hour, I would report her to the Infirmary and hint to the Police—picked some parts of cinder from the lower parts of her body—applied to have her to the Infirmary, and was successful—helped her—she took half an hour—might have gone in two minutes but from her weakness.

This statement was borne out in all its parts by Mrs Godin, Dr. Stirling, the Nurse, Clerk, and Surgeon of the Infirmary, and many other witnesses. The prisoner was unanimously found Guilty, and after an impressive address from the Lord Justice Clerk, who characterised this crime as the most atrocious case of brutal cruelty and savage barbarity that had ever come under his observation, sentenced him to be Executed on the 7th November, between the hours of 2 and 4, and his body buried within the precincts of the jail.

Agreeably to this sentence, the prisoner was brought to the scaffold at the hour appointed, attended by the Clergy of the persuasion he belonged to, and after spending a short time in prayer on the fatal drop, it fell and in a few moments he became a lifeless corpse. After the body had been suspended the usual time, it was cut down and conveyed back to the jail, for the purpose of being buried within its precincts, in terms of the new Act.

Since his conviction, he conducted himself in a manner becoming his awful situation, and the horrid nature of the crime he had to atone for.— He was very penitent and resigned, and ascribes all his past misconduct to the effects arising from intemperance, which made him callous to every feeling of humanity—caused him to ill-use and cruelly beat his wife—and at length led him to commit that horrid crime which the laws of his country could visit with no other punishment than death.

He professed to believe in the tenets of the Church of Rome, (though in practice, as well as persons of all sects,) he grossly perverted them. He was assisted in his religious exercises by the Reverend Bishop Scott, the Rev. Mr. Murdoch, &c. to whose instructions and admonitions he listened with the utmost attention and eagerness.

He originally belonged to a place called Green Castle in Ireland, but has been residing in this country some number of years, and, has lived a considerable time in Drygate Street, the place where the murder was perpetrated. He was a man of low stature, about 45 years of age, and his employment was cleaning of closes and emptying of dungsteads, or any other out-door work. He has left a daughter about 14 years old.

A crime, perpetrated with such horrid brutality, has seldom been recorded, and we trust will never occur again. It ought to be a warning to drunkards, to persons of hasty passion, and to old and young—'for all need advice.

Wm. Carse, Printer, Glasgow.

Newspaper report of the George Duffy execution.

Before his execution took place George apparently became penitent, blaming his heavy drinking for the appalling behaviour towards his wife. The Reverends Scott and Murdoch were his confidants and listened to his soul searching confession. Too little too late. George was led away to the gallows and duly hanged, his body allowed to dangle for the usual time and then cut down and buried within the prison walls as decreed by Lord Justice Clerk – with no ceremony as befitted his crime. It can truly be said the downfall of George Duffy and his entire family was the result of his foul temper brought on by his excessive drinking. His actions not only brought about the death of his wife and himself but left their fourteen-year-old daughter parentless.

CHAPTER 4

The Perils of Drink: Hans MacFarlane, Helen Blackwood & Mary Hamilton

1835

Wherever you lived in the city (not exclusively Glasgow) during the early part of the nineteenth century, unless you were part of the gentry, you were more than likely to live within or close to overcrowded areas of squalor. The River Clyde has always provided a positive source of income, enhancing the local economy by creating employment and therefore attracting people to come and work and live in the city. With that came overcrowding as the ever expanding urban conurbations could not handle the quantity of immigrants coming into Glasgow. In the worst areas, houses were split into rooms and rented out, tiny and rat infested living spaces. It is said that in some rooms up to three families would live, that's (on average) twelve people crammed into a compact area, offering no privacy and even less in the way of sanitary conditions or running water. In some cases, the rooms were the ideal premises to run brothels or 'low dens' as they were then called in the city. Imagine then, several women, prostitutes working from a room that measured eight feet by six feet and four inches. With one bed to share between them the sexual activities that took place were more like public performances than private sexual acts.

In June 1835, two men, Alexander Boyd and James Law, both working as ship carpenters, were out on the town. They had inadvertently bumped into each other and decided to hit the drink and recount old times and encounters. For much of

Shipbuilding crane on River Clyde. It was an industry that attracted many immigrants.

the afternoon of Saturday 13 June 1835, the two men spent time in various hostelries and inns, consuming copious amounts of ale. The drink binge continued into the early hours of Sunday 14 June 1835, by which time both men were extremely merry and game for anything. They moved on to the New Vennel area and there, at about 1.00 am, found themselves accosted by a small group of loose women, all keen to please the men and to 'service' them. James Law needed no encouragement and agreed to go with the women for a bit of fun. Alexander Boyd meanwhile was probably the less drunk of the pair and, knowing some of the horrendous assaults and crimes that take place in such low dens, was more reluctant to go with the women. Eventually, peer pressure told and James Law and the prostitutes managed to get him to come along.

This particular den of iniquity was owned and managed by a hard-faced and emotionally cold woman called Helen Blackwood who was gracious and welcoming to the two men as they entered her premises. Immediately, the liquor began to flow and some of the niceties between the men and the prostitutes took place; a bit of kissing and progressed into the men wanting more serious sexual activity. James Law wasn't handling the situation well, he seemed to be greatly affected by the liquor he was drinking in the house. There was a reason for this. It was likely he had been drugged.

Boyd on the other hand, still had partial control of his senses and managed to keep his wits about him. As both men sat on the bed in the tiny room two of the women began undressing James Law. As they removed his clothes another woman was going through the pockets, removing any money, jewellery or any valuables that could be sold on. Laws offered no resistance.

The prostitutes had been joined in the room by a man and woman. The man was Hans Smith MacFarlane, the partner of Helen Blackwood; and with him was Mary Hamilton. They were undoubtedly the main inspiration behind what was clearly theft. MacFarlane's appearance resulted in a more rugged and violent treatment of the two men. Boyd was going to have none of it, though he was far too drunk to defend himself appropriately. He resisted the efforts of the women to undress him and fought bravely, but was overwhelmed when MacFarlane became involved. Unable to further prevent the attack, Boyd was systematically relieved of his clothing and valuables. He remonstrated and shouted at the group, threatening to call the police.

Hans MacFarlane aided and coaxed on by Helen Blackwood and Mary Hamilton, then told the two women to take hold of the prostrate Boyd and to help him carry him over to the window. The window, which was three stories from the street, around twenty-six feet, was opened. Boyd was carried over to it and tossed out head first, landing on the back of his head which impacted against cobbled street below. Blood and brain tissue oozed from the fractured skull. Alexander Boyd was dead, murdered by a wicked trio because he protested too much.

Elsewhere in the room were two young boys, one aged fourteen and the other only ten. Generally the children were told to secrete themselves beneath the bed when a customer came back to the room, where there they remained while sex acts were performed just a few inches above them. The boys were there when Alexander Boyd was murdered, they witnessed everything, their presence seemingly forgotten in the excitement of the situation. The children were not the only witnesses, a group of other women who lived in other rooms within the house had heard the commotion being made by Boyd. Curiously, they had gone to the room where the noise emanated from. Looking through a hole in the door they peered inside and saw the entire drama of murder unfold. At once they screamed, running down the stairs and into the street to see if they could help the poor man who had been precipitated through the window. Their screams and shouts for help soon aroused the interest of the police who under the leadership of Captain Mackay took in descriptions and other details of the crime. The three persons responsible had absconded, fleeing the scene once the screams were cried out. Mackay had descriptions of the perpetrators disseminated to police stations in the district. A number of officers were instructed to watch upon every portion of the principality. Others were instructed to search the neighbourhood and to arrest the trio.

Mary Hamilton had split from MacFarlane and Blackwood and was soon under lock and key having been detained in High Street.

Several hours later, between 5am and 6.00 am, the two other absentees were arrested as they crossed some open land in Bridgeton. MacFarlane denied any involvement, claiming that it was a case of mistaken identity. A search of his clothes soon ended such claims when personal property belonging to both Law and Boyd was found in his pockets. He stated he had purchased these from a man in an inn whose identity was unknown to him. Helen Blackwood denied being such a person and said she had no knowledge of a low den in New Vennel. Again, personal property belonging to James Law was found on her. The pair were incarcerated whilst the police investigated the matter further.

Witness identification and information provided a solid case against the murderous trio. The two young boys told of what had happened as did the women who had seen the crime take place through the door. Other persons came forward speaking of similar experiences, albeit without murder, when visiting the premises. James Law provided some background information on Alexander Boyd, but could recall nothing of the crime or the incidents within the rooms. It was later agreed that the liquor they were consuming was drugged in order to make them insensible and easy to steal from.

Law stated that the deceased man was about forty years of age, strong in build and very honest in character. He had previously been living in Valpraiso and had come to Scotland in March 1835 to care for some property that he had inherited in Edinburgh, as a consequence of his mother's death in that city. He had taken temporary lodgings in Finnieston Lane and when Law had come across him, he stated his intention to travel to Dumbarton. The subsequent trial was a straight forward affair, the guilt of the trio never in doubt. As for James Law, one can only hope the he learned of the perils of alcohol after this despicable episode.

Chapter 5

Who Hacked Poor Jessie to Death?
Jessie McLachlan

1862

If ever a case was decided by the class of the people involved, then this is it. It involved Jessie McPherson, a servant girl to an accountant and his elderly father, John Fleming, his son John junior and James Fleming senior. They lived at 17 Sandyford Place in Glasgow in relative respectability and comfort. James Fleming, although aged eighty-seven, still had his wits about him and an ardour that he found difficult to suppress when Jessie was around. There can be no doubt, with his son frequently away on work and with alcohol playing its part, that James was tempted by the close proximity of Jess, aged thirty-five and a comely lass.

James had been a handloom weaver in Kilsyth and, having worked hard, found himself in a position to open his own weaving business with all the responsibility and prosperity that came with it. He had been in a position to give his own son a good education and the boy had become an accountant. Not wishing to seem ungrateful to his father the widowed John Fleming had his father living with him and even gave him £40 a year to collect rents on some property for him. All in all the Flemings were an upstanding family of the community.

Jess McPherson on the other hand had received no such upbringing and had found herself mother to two illegitimate children, one of which was stillborn. She was known to enjoy a dalliance and had once teased a policeman who, on trying to kiss her, had found himself thrown upon the floor, lured by Jess but then rejected. Jess would not have had much choice about the type of work she could expect to be employed at, not being trained in a profession as such and so it was fortuitous when she was given the position as servant girl in John Flemings household.

The trouble started when John Fleming and his son went to Dunoon for the weekend of Friday 4 July 1862, leaving Jess McPherson and old James Fleming alone in the house. They would not have been concerned about this state of affairs as although Jess had confided to friends about the elder Flemings amorous advances towards her, she had not mentioned this to her employer. Father and son had a pleasant trip and returned refreshed and ready for a hard week's work back in Glasgow on Monday 7 July. They had gone straight to their office in St Vincent Place and worked until the afternoon when they then separated on the journey home, the father stopping off to get some food for their dinner and the son travelling on home. When John junior arrived at Sandyford Place the door was opened not by Jess as he would have expected, but by his grandfather, who explained that Jess had gone away. James also curiously mentioned that the door of Jess's room was locked. Before young John could establish further details, the food his father had purchased turned up, delivered by the butcher boy. Young John, seeing his father following, remarked the futility of having any food when there was no servant girl to cook it.

John Fleming senior, fetching the key to Jess's room on the way, led the party to the locked door and opened it. The room was dark and lying on the bed was Jess McPherson, her clothes removed from her lower body and clearly dead. It was left to the butcher boy to call for a doctor who ascertained she had been dead for some time.

Every place has its share of nosy busy bodies and this area of Glasgow was no different. It came in the form of Mrs Walker, the wife of a grocer who by chance happened to be looking out of her window and was witness to a policeman running into her husband's shop. Curiosity no stranger to her, Mrs Walker set out to find the reason for this commotion and was rewarded with the knowledge that a servant girl had been found dead in a basement at 17 Sandyford Place. Using the excuse to provide the policeman with matches for the candle he had borrowed from the shop she hurried herself off to the basement. The discussion at the house revolved around old James Fleming having said that Jess had been away but not thinking to find when and if Jess had returned because her door was locked. Mrs Walker became super sleuth and asked if he had heard any noises from the room at any time, to which he had replied that he had heard moaning noises about four o'clock on the Saturday morning and that he had thought nothing of it. Mrs Walker had found this extraordinary that being the only other person in the house he did not see fit to establish the source of the noises. Eventually, with an already contaminated crime scene, the police surgeon arrived and ascertained that Jess had been brutally hit about the head and arms with either an axe or a cleaver. The washing of parts of Jess's room and the kitchen also became apparent and three naked footprints in Jess's blood were now noticed on the floor. The basement area seems to have been in some disarray with blood in various areas, on clothes in Jess's room and on some shirts of James Fleming's. John Fleming senior discovered that some silver plate was missing and also that Jess's chest had been rifled with all her best dresses gone, evidently sorted

Murder victim Jessie McLachlan.

through by a bloody hand. The post-mortem showed that the injuries inflicted on Jess had been dealt by a weak man or a woman. James Fleming fitted the weak man scenario, but who could have been the woman?

A description of the missing plate was circulated in the papers along with news of the gory death and a pawnbroker by the name of Robert Lundie read this description and realised he had taken in the very same silver plate at his shop and his records revealed that it had been a Mary McDonald who had pawned the items, receiving £6.15s in payment. It became clear to the police that both the name and address given by the woman, Mary McDonald, had been false and, armed only with a description, they could be forgiven for thinking this may have been the end of the trail. However, at this time James Fleming had been arrested and questioned by the Sheriff and committed to prison. Amazingly, after his incarceration, the police said they were informed by an unknown person of both

Old Fleming – did he kill Jessie McLachlan?

the address and name of the woman they sought. This led them to 182 Broomielaw and a twenty-eight-year-old woman known as Mrs Jessie McLachlan. She was married to a sailor who was away on a cargo ship and had been a close friend of the murdered girl and James Fleming. Jessie and her husband on his return from sea were duly arrested, Mr McLachlan being released when it was realised he was not even on land at the time of the murder. Jessie was repeatedly questioned about her involvement with Jess's death and eventually imprisoned to await trial. During this time Jessie gave several statements, the first taking four and a half hours to complete:

'My name is Jessie McIntosh or McLachlan, I am a native of Inverness, twenty-eight years of age, wife of James McLachlan, second mate on board the steamship *Pladda,* and I reside at No 182 Broomielaw, Glasgow. I knew Jessie McPherson, who was a servant to Mr Fleming, Sandyford Place, Sauchiehall Road. I was a fellow servant of hers in Mr Fleming's employment in his house at Sandyford Place, and at his coast house near Dunoon, for two years prior to September 1857. I left Mr Fleming's service then and got married, and since then I have kept intimacy with her, except for a period of about eighteen months prior to January 1861, during which time she was at service in Manchester.'

'I last saw Jessie McPherson in my own house at the Broomielaw on Saturday evening the 28th June last. I had also seen her the previous night at Mrs Fleming's house at Sandyford Place, and I went there about ten o'clock. I rang the front door bell, but Jessie McPherson happened to be in the dining-room, and she told me to go round the lane behind the house and she would let me in by the back door. I went round and found the back door open, and Jessie McPherson speaking to a servant in the adjoining house, No 16 Sandyford Place. McPherson and I left this girl in the lane and went inside the back door; we conversed there about McPherson going to New Zealand, which she had previously told me she intended to do. That night I went by appointment to see her on this subject. McPherson asked me to get a schedule from an emigration society in Jamaica Street that it might be filled up for her. I did not get the schedule when I applied for it, and it was to see if I had got it that McPherson came to my house, the last time I saw her on said Saturday night.'

'I was not in or near Mr Fleming's house on the evening of Friday the 4th, or the morning of Saturday the 5th of the current month of July, and did see Jessie McPherson that night or morning, and I was in no way concerned in assaulting or murdering her, nor was I concerned in stealing any silver plate from McPherson's house on said night or morning.'

'On said Friday the 4th July I was in my house the whole day till about seven o'clock at night, when I went to see Mr McFarlane who had been factor for my house prior to Whitsunday, and whose place of business was a 112 West George Street, but he was not within, whereupon I returned home. I was not again out of my house till after ten o'clock, when I went out to convoy home a Mrs Fraser, a seaman's wife who lives in Grace Street, Anderston. I walked with her as far as the Gushet House in Anderston where I parted from her. I intended to go to the house of James McGregor, a foreman clothier, who lives in Main Street, Anderston, and who is a friend of my husband's but I changed my mind and returned home by way of Argyle Street, James Watt Street and Broomielaw. I reached home about a quarter past eleven o'clock; I let myself in by means of a check lock key and which is in the house; this key I carried myself and always let myself in by means of it; it is one of the keys of the press in the lobby of my house, and for which press there are two keys.'

'On going upstairs I found John McDonald, a young man who lodged with Mrs Campbell, who occupied a part of my house. He was going upstairs before me and went into the house along with me, he did not remain in the house above a minute, then went out again. I went straight to bed without speaking to Mrs Campbell, but in about half an hour I heard the door bell ring and Mrs Campbell opened the door and I heard from the voice that it was McDonald returning. I remained in bed until between seven and eight o'clock on Saturday morning without ever having been up or out of the house. My son, a child of three years of age, slept in bed with me.'

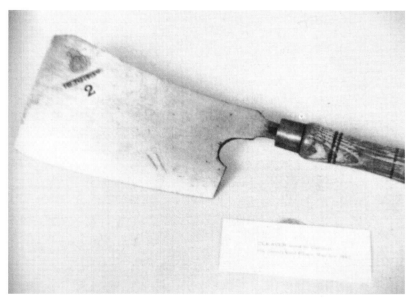

Hatchet that killed poor Jessie.

'When I rose I dressed and went out without breakfast leaving my child in bed. I went for coals to the house of an old woman in West College Street. I brought back the coals in a large basket covered with a piece of old carpet which I had taken out with me. I was absent above a quarter of an hour. Mrs Campbell was not up and out of bed when I went out but she was out of bed when I returned because I rang the bell and she let me in. I had forgotten to take the check key with me. Mrs Campbell had taken my child out of my bed and dressed him while I was absent. I lighted my fire and made a breakfast for myself and child.'

'I remained in the house until about twelve o'clock on the said Saturday, when I went out and went to the pawn office of Mr Lundie in East Clyde Street. I went there to pawn silver plate which I had received from Mr James Fleming, the father of Mr Fleming, my late master on the previous evening in my house. He came to my house about a quarter past eight that evening and I let him in and took him into our parlour. He carried a parcel wrapped tightly up in a white cloth and laid it down on the table. He asked me if I would go a message for him and he would pay me well for it.'

'I asked him what it was and he said he wanted me to pawn some silver plate which was in the parcel. I said the pawnbroker would know the plate did not belong to me. He said I was to say it was rent I had to pay. I asked what name I would give as a pledger, and if I would give Mr Fleming's name and he said no, not to put down Mr Fleming's name as it would be in the directory. I then said: "What name will I give?" and he said I was to give the name of Mary McKay or McDonald, No 5 or No 35 St Vincent Street and that I was to seek £3.10s upon the plate or as much more as I could get. Fleming said that he was short of money and had to go to the Highlands and id not like to lift the money out of the bank. I agreed to pawn the plate and Fleming said he would come and see me next afternoon and then he left the house. There was no one with Fleming and me in the parlour and I do not know that anyone saw him in the house; but Mrs Campbell was in at the time he was there.'

'I went as I have already said to Lundie's pawn office and it was then between twelve and one o'clock on the Saturday. I laid down the parcel, rolled up as old Mr Fleming had given it to me. The pawnbroker's young man who attended me opened down the parcel and then it was I saw for the first time what the parcel contained. The young man asked me what I wanted on the articles and I said £3 10s, and he said he would give me a little more then that and I said I would take as much as he would give me as the articles would not lie long in pawn. He said he would give me £6 10s or £6 15s, I forget which. I told the young man that the money was wanted to pay rent, but I did not say who sent me. I gave as the pledger's name Mary McKay or McDonald as Old Fleming had told me.'

'I got the money and a pawn ticket and left he silver plate in the same cover which Old Fleming had brought the particle in. I saw when the parcel was opened down by the pawnbroker that the articles consisted of a soup divider, a fish slice, some table spoons and forks and toddy ladles. I knew the silver articles when I was a servant in the house and saw them sufficiently well in the pawnbroker's hands to know them again.'

'I returned straight home from the pawn office with the money and ticket and reached home about a quarter past one. I remained in the houses and at about a quarter to three Fleming came there. I was a the moment cleaning the brasses of the door and he and I turned into the parlour. He then asked me if I had got his message and I told him I had got more than he thought and then gave him the whole money I had got, together with the pawn ticket. He thereupon offered me £5 for having done the message and not to mention it to any person. I told him that £5 was too much for me and I took £4 from him. Fleming repeated that I was to tell no one of what I had done for him in case it would come to his son's ears, and that a pound or two would do him when he was away in the Highlands. On this Fleming left the house.'

'I had promised Mr Caldwell the present factor of my house £4 on Friday the previous day and so on getting the £4 from Fleming I went and paid the whole of it to Caldwell about four o'clock on Saturday.'

'I am shown a man who calls himself James Fleming and I declare and identify that man as the person who gave me said silver plate to pawn on said Friday and to whom I gave the money and pawn ticket on the Saturday.'

'I had money of my own wherewith to pay the factor on the Friday independent of the £4 which I got from Fleming on Saturday. I had £5 10s of my own in the house which was a balance of £11 10s which I got from my brother in the end of May last. My brother's name is John McIntosh. He was a seaman on board the steamship *St George* which plied between Glasgow and Quebec.'

'On Friday night the 4th July, when I went to convoy Mrs Fraser I was dressed in a brown merino dress with three flounces, a large light grey cloth cloak and a brown velvet bonnet. On Saturday the 5th July I took the grey cloak to Mr Murray the dyer's shop in Argyle Street that I might be cleaned where a the same time I left the brown merino dress to be dyed black. I gave my own name Mrs McLachlan to Mr Murray as the owner.'

'I took the velvet off the frame of the said bonnet because it was old and I it to a salt and whiting girl at the door of my house on Tuesday last. I had a brown merino dress without flounces, but I gave the skirt of it to Mary Black or Adams, a washerwoman, last summer. I did not open down the brown merino dress left to be dyed.'

'The washerwoman just mentioned has been in the habit of washing for me about three years past. She did not call for me at my house in the afternoon or evening of Friday, 4th July. I did not ask Mary Black or Adams to come to my house and take charge of my son James while I went and saw the late Jessie McPherson on said Friday night.'

'Mary Black or Adams stays with Mrs Rainny in Holm Street. I called once there on Saturday the 5th July. I wanted Adams to go a message but she was not in and Mrs Rainny said she would go the message. The message was to redeem from a pawnbroker a black and blue check poplin dress and which I now have on as under dress and Mrs Rainny relieved and brought me the dress. I wore the brown dress at this time not having sent it to the dyeing. I left word for Mary Adams to be sent to my house that Saturday afternoon and she came. I gave her two £1 notes to redeem other articles from the pawn. On the Monday following I gave her 11s to redeem some other articles which were pledged. I gave her no more money.'

'I had two crinolines on Friday and Saturday the 4th and 5th July. I have now only one the other having been burnt by accident on Saturday 5th July. The wires of that crinoline I gave to Mary Adams. I purchased a new black straw bonnet on Wednesday last, the 9th in a milliner's shop in Argyle Street. I paid 4s9d for it.'

'Mary Adams has a younger daughter named Sarah. I sent her with a box to the Hamilton railway on Saturday the 5th July. I addressed it with the name "Mrs Bain, Hamilton. To lie till called for". The box was empty. I intended to go up to Hamilton on said Saturday and stay for a day or two with a Mrs Shaw there but who I through mistake understood was called Mrs Bain. I did not go on Saturday but went on Tuesday last and called at Mrs Shaw's house and found she was not within. I got said box at the Hamilton station on said day and returned home with it reaching Glasgow about six o'clock on Tuesday night. The box is now in the house. It is a leather box with a glazed cover. I meant the empty box to lie at the Glasgow station till I went myself to Hamilton, but through some mistake of the little girl Adams it had been sent on to Hamilton. I meant to have put my clothes in the box at the station, because the little girl could not carry the box and clothes together. I carried my clothes across to the Glasgow station of the railway in a black leather bag and which I took to Hamilton when I found the box had been sent forward.'

'I am shown and identify as my property two sheets. My attention is called to the mark or impression of a key appearing on one of said sheets. I declare that the impression was made upwards of twelve months ago, and while I resided in a house at Stobcross Street. The impression is of the check key of the outer door of that house, and was made by my child making water on it as it lay on the sheet, which left an impression of the key in iron mould on the sheet. My sister, Ann McIntosh, who now resides at Garnethill in Edinburgh, knew of said occurrence.'

'I am shown and identify as my property a chemise and flannel petticoat, both of which I was wearing when I was taken into custody yesterday. I put on said chemise and petticoat on the evening of Thursday the 3rd July. I had two chemises but one of which I have since put on. That now shown to me I have torn up having been destroyed by my child. I had no flannel petticoat except that now shown me. I washed it on Wednesday the day before I put it on.'

'I was indebted to the late Jessie McPherson in the sum of £1 5s for grocery goods which I got from her when she kept a shop in Grace Street about two years ago. This sum I did not pay because McPherson told me that she meant to have made a present to my child at its birth and that I was to retain the money and expend it for the child.'

'On being shown a black shawl or plaid that is not my property and I never had it in my possession and I did not leave it at Murrays before mentioned, to be dipped in black dye, on Monday last nor did I send it. Being also shown a grey cloth cloak in two pieces – I declare that is the cloak which I wore on Friday and Saturday the 4th and 5th July and which has now been cleaned, but it was not in pieces when I gave it to be cleaned. I am shown the bodice and skirt of a dress new dyed black. I declare that it is the brown dress which I wore on said Friday and Saturday now dyed black and which as shown me want the flounces. I did not give the name McDonald to Murray as owner of said cloth cloak and brown dress. I gave my own name McLachlan. I got from the dyer a ticket on leaving said articles which I suppose is now somewhere about the house. I dyed said dress black to get further use out of it as in its brown state it was a good deal soiled and the colour faded.'

'All which I declare to be truth.'

An exhaustive statement and one of five made by Jessie. Much of the above is untrue and was easily disproved by the police. It was known that Jessie was out of her house all of the night of the 4th and 5 July. Jessie did not, as she stated have a key to her house which is why Mrs Campbell had to let her in, it was also known that she had been wearing the brown dress with flounces on Friday night and that this had changed into a different dress when Mrs Campbell opened the door to her on Saturday morning. The police, under Superintendent McCall, worked uncharacteristically hard after taking Jessie's statement and were rewarded on Wednesday 16th July by James McLachlan who told them of a second black box to be found at Bridge Street railway station. Within this box were the clothes missing from Jessie McPherson's chest. When presented with this incriminating evidence Jessie McLachlan wove another web of lies and non truths. She said that Jessie McPherson had sent the clothes to her with instructions to take the dresses to Anderson in Buchanan Street for dressing and dyeing and the cloak also. This had taken place on Friday afternoon. Jessie McLachlan said that she had not had time to run the errands for her friend and when she heard that Jess's clothes were missing became panicked as they were in her possession and so she had sent them to Ayr and addressed the box to 'Mrs Darnley'. Jessie's husband knew all about this because she had told him of her intentions and on hearing of Jess's death had asked him to retrieve the box from Ayr and take it to Greenock. She said her husband had wanted her to tell the Fiscal but she had been too frightened.

Jessie had reason to be frightened, for on the same day Dr George Macleod came to her in prison and requested her help in a small experiment. He persuaded her to place her foot in bullock's blood and then to step onto a piece of wooden plank thereby leaving a print of her footstep. Amazingly Jessie agreed to this and managed to incriminate herself all the more as the doctor declared the footprint to be a match for those found in Jess McPherson's room 'with a degree of accuracy which was quite marvellous'. Whilst Jessie was sinking lower into the mire, the Fiscal who was acquainted with the Fleming family arranged for old James Fleming to be released from prison without charge, this despite his being possibly one of the two principal suspects. Jessie McLachlan alone was officially charged with murder and theft.

Jessie understandably was none too pleased when informed about this turn of events, but even as she was accusing old Mr Fleming of the murder the police were discovering further evidence in the form of pieces of clothing in fields near Low Waters, not far from town. The pieces were identified as Jessie McLachlan's and they were heavily bloodstained, at the very least putting her in the vicinity of the crime. The newspapers of the day made a good deal of the information leaked their way and circulation for one paper was said to have risen from 10,000 to 50,000 a day. This public attention to the crime made it a fairly sure bet that Jessie McLachlan was not going to get a fair trial.

On 17 September the court was in session for the beginning of Jessie's trial, Lord Death, real name Lord Deas, was the presiding judge, with a strong penchant for capital punishment, so what chance did Jessie McLachlan have? Old Mr Fleming was called to the witness stand and gave a strong performance, even the small matter of why, when the milk boy called on the Saturday morning he answered the door himself, fully dressed, and did not wait for Jess McPherson to take the call, as would have been usual, did not deter him. His replies were hard to make sense of but it is thought that he referred to 'we', as in 'we knew it was over for Jess by then'. Did he know she was already dead? and who was with him? He had denied before the trial that he ever knew Jessie McLachlan but now admitted that he did know the girl and had visited her house? Despite many discrepancies in his evidence old Mr Fleming had the judge to protect him and the defence was cut off many times as he was attempting to make pertinent points and when he tried to enter into court the reputation of old Mr Fleming's lecherous ways which had seen him being called before the kirk, Lord Deas declared that 'this need not be opened up just now with the witness'. The judge's summing up of the case was biased heavily against Jessie McLachlan and, as he had already brought his black cap with him, there can be little doubt as to how he saw the verdict.

Fifteen minutes after leaving the court the jury were back with a guilty verdict. The prospect of languishing in jail prompted Jessie to make her final statement which no doubt had more truthful elements than her previous ones. She told a tale of how she had arrived at Sandyford Place to find Jess McPherson and old Mr Fleming already drinking and that Jess was complaining about his amorous advances to her, having gone to fetch more drink, Jessie returned to find that her friend had been battered about the head by Mr Fleming and was in a bad way, he had persuaded her to help him and she had used her clothes to wipe Jess's wounds. Together, Jessie and Mr Fleming had put Jess to bed, but on realising her friend was in need of a doctor she left them alone and made her way to the front door, which she found locked. On returning to Jess's room, old Mr Fleming persuaded her to wait till morning as he was ashamed of the damage he had done. Jessie went upstairs and when she came back down again found old Mr Fleming striking Jess about the head and upper body with a meat cleaver. Having been warned by Fleming that she was now implicated in the crime she helped him to clean up the scene, using both her own and his clothes to mop up the mess, and in the process leaving her telltale footprints in her friend's blood. Fleming had then given her the silver plate to pawn and instructed her to use a fictitious name so that she could not be traced. This would make the scene resemble a murder after a robbery gone wrong. Lord Deas did what he did best and sentenced Jessie to death by hanging. However such was the public outcry against this, and the doubt in many people's minds as to the fairness of the trial that the sentence was commuted to life imprisonment. Jessie Mclachlan spent the obligatory fifteen years in jail and was released on 5 Oct 5 1877 whereupon herself and her son finally travelled to Michigan in the United States of America and where she died in Port Huron in 1899.

Why was old Mr Fleming never called to answer for his many glaring inconsistencies? Probably because he was an educated wealthy member of the community and to put him on trial would be like putting the established upper class on trial and that would never have happened, not while an uneducated poor servant woman was available to take the fall. We may never know for sure who actually killed poor Jess McPherson, but it seems to me that old Mr Fleming had a reputation and his son's benevolence to lose, in those days powerful motives. Jessie McLachlan had not tried to conceal herself when she visited her friend and apart from ongoing poverty had very little motive to kill. Only Jess McPherson knows the whole truth and she cannot tell us.

CHAPTER 6

A Peculiar Case of Murder: Oscar Slater

1908

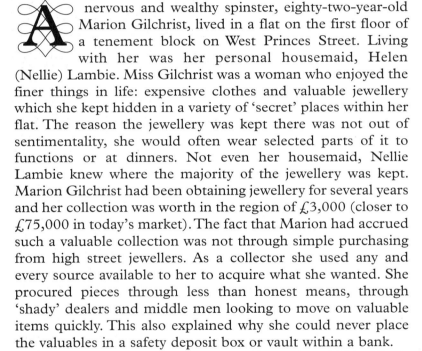

A nervous and wealthy spinster, eighty-two-year-old Marion Gilchrist, lived in a flat on the first floor of a tenement block on West Princes Street. Living with her was her personal housemaid, Helen (Nellie) Lambie. Miss Gilchrist was a woman who enjoyed the finer things in life: expensive clothes and valuable jewellery which she kept hidden in a variety of 'secret' places within her flat. The reason the jewellery was kept there was not out of sentimentality, she would often wear selected parts of it to functions or at dinners. Not even her housemaid, Nellie Lambie knew where the majority of the jewellery was kept. Marion Gilchrist had been obtaining jewellery for several years and her collection was worth in the region of £3,000 (closer to £75,000 in today's market). The fact that Marion had accrued such a valuable collection was not through simple purchasing from high street jewellers. As a collector she used any and every source available to her to acquire what she wanted. She procured pieces through less than honest means, through 'shady' dealers and middle men looking to move on valuable items quickly. This also explained why she could never place the valuables in a safety deposit box or vault within a bank.

Shortly before 7.00 pm, on 21 December 1908, Nellie Lambie had popped out of the flat for around ten minutes, to buy a newspaper for her mistress. In the flat immediately below Marion Gilchrist's lived the Adams family. Arthur Adams was in the dining room of his home when he heard peculiar noises coming from the flat above. This was unusual as generally Miss Gilchrist and her maid were very quiet. The

Marion Gilchrist.

first noise was a heavy and loud thump; this was followed by three knocks. Adams was concerned as some time earlier he had been in conversation with Marion Gilchrist who openly confessed to being more than a little paranoid that – as a wealthy woman living with a maid – she was vulnerable to burglars who would want to steal her jewellery and valuables. Adams had agreed that should he ever hear anything suspicious and out of the ordinary in or around Marion's flat he would come up to check out that all was well. Certainly, the unusual noises he heard that evening were suspicious. He left the sanctuary of his own flat and climbed the stairs leading to Marion's. At the entrance door to the apartment he heard more strange noises from within, like the sound of someone chopping sticks. He rang the doorbell several times but was unable to illicit a response, then went back down to his own flat. There his sister demanded that he go back to the upstairs flat and speak to Marion to check all was well, as the noises had continued. Again he climbed the stairs. This time, as he reached Marion's flat he heard the sound of someone else coming up the stairs, and was shocked to see that it was Nellie Lambie. As the pair opened the door of the flat and moved inside, a well dressed and furtive man rushed out of a room on

Scene of Marion Gilchrist murder.

the right; he moved swiftly, pausing for a moment close to
Arthur Adams, as though he was going to speak to him, then
quickly moved past him, down the stairs and disappeared out
into the street. Adams jumped in fright at the man's
emergence from the room (it was a bedroom); however, Nellie
Lambie didn't at all appear phased by the man's presence.
Nellie first checked the kitchen, but the suspicions of Arthur
Adams had been aroused, and he wanted to find Marion
Gilchrist to check that she was safe.

Nellie Adams seemed a little reticent to search the rooms.
Arthur told her to go to the dining room since that was the
room where the noises he had heard appeared to be coming
from (the dining room was situated immediately above that of
Arthur Adam's flat). On entering the room, Nellie Lambie let
out a scream and stood rooted to the spot. Arthur Adams
rushed to the scene and saw, laid in front of the fire, the body
of Marion Gilchrist. Her head had been hastily covered by a
rug. It had been bludgeoned and was a mass of blood. Without
further ado, Arthur Adams ran out of the flat and went in

Marion Gilchrist apartment block.

search of the man who he had seen leaving. Running out into the street below, he found no trace of the man in the immediate vicinity. On his return, the police had arrived at the flat. The policeman was more concerned with the state of Marion Gilchrist than any offender, a good thing too as he noticed that she was still breathing. A local physician, Dr Adams (no relation to Arthur Adams) was summoned but by the time he arrived Marion Gilchrist was dead as a result of the injuries to her head. The doctor observed a chair that lay nearby. It was covered in blood, so he declared that this was in all probability the murder weapon.

Shortly after, a team of detectives arrived at the scene and began the painstaking task of speaking to witnesses and putting together all the information they could find in order to identify the culprit and a motive.

Of course, it didn't take them long to learn of Marion Gilchrist's expensive collecting habits resulting in the discovery a gas lamp that had been lit in a spare bedroom. Below this was a box of matches found close by on a table,

Inside the murder apartment.

not of the make used in the flat. Also on the table was a toilet dish containing some smaller pieces of jewellery. There was a wooden box that had clearly been forced open. Inside it were some personal papers, the rest of its contents strewn across the floor. A gold pocket watch and chain was also on the table. Nellie Lambie confirmed that the only item she could see missing was a crescent-shaped gold and diamond brooch.

The police were also very keen to identify the mysterious man seen leaving the flat and hurrying out of the tenement block. The one curious point that they noticed was that there was no sign of forced entry, meaning Marion Gilchrist may have unwittingly let her killer into the flat. Arthur Adams was vociferous in his condemnation of this speculation, claiming that Marion was far too nervous to allow a stranger access. Other witnesses, neighbours, described seeing a man loitering in the street outside; this differed from the description offered by Arthur Adams. A fourteen-year-old girl, Mary Barrowman, informed the police that she had been in the area close to the

Oscar Salter.

time of the murder and had actually bumped into a man hurriedly leaving Marion Gilchrist's address. The man both Adams and Lambie described was 'about 5′ 6″ tall, dark and wearing a light grey overcoat and a black cap'. The man Mary Barrowman described was 'tall, young, with a fawn cloak and a round hat'.

On Christmas Day, a man came forward and told the police that a person he knew as 'Oscar', who was a fellow member of a club in India Street, had been trying to sell a pawn ticket that related to a diamond crescent shaped brooch. Oscar lived at number 69 George Street.

Oscar Slater was a German Jew and a petty criminal. Slater was known to the police as a keen gambler and was also known to run illegal gambling-dens; and also bought and sold jewellery of all kinds. He had been staying in George Street, Glasgow, not too far from the Gilchrist residence. He lived with a woman of highly dubious character who called herself Madame Andree Junio Antoine. By the time the police visited 69 George Street, both Slater and Antoine had fled the country on the same Christmas Day, making their way to Liverpool where they took the ocean liner *Lusitania* to New York. It was known and expected that both fleeing suspects would use aliases and try to change their appearance.

A description and details of the wanted man were telegraphed to the New York authorities and, when the ship docked, Slater was apprehended and detained at the quayside. He had with him in his possession a small upholster's hammer. Later, this item was produced as a police exhibit, a potential murder weapon. Oscar Slater denied his involvement, and in an attempt to prove his innocence offered to cooperate and help the authorities with their investigations. He actually waived extradition (just as well as their was insufficient evidence to have him extradited) and agreed to return to Scotland. Slater was, he himself claimed, an innocent man and had nothing to fear in returning to Glasgow.

In Glasgow, he provided an alibi for the crucial time of the murder. Further to this, in an attempt to justify why he and his partner were travelling under false names, he said that this was done in order that his estranged wife could not track him down. So far as the pawn ticket evidence went, he admitted to trying to sell such an item long before the murder occurred. It was something that he readily tried to do in order to move on items of jewellery.

Despite facts that seemed to contradict the official police evidence, Slater was charged with murder and brought to trial in Edinburgh on 3 May 1909. He incorrectly believed that he would be given a fair hearing and that his alibi's were cast iron, proving without doubt, his innocence in the entire matter. The peculiar fact that Slater continued to believe that the murder occurred on 22 December 1908, was lost on the investigating police. As the crime took place on the night of 21 December 1908, would Slater, if guilty of the crime, forget the date he took someone's life so brutally? The case against him was hardly watertight, for a man charged with murder it has to be said there was very little in the way of actual evidence. The trial was a sham. Some of the witnesses were keen to claim their share of the £200 reward on offer for the information leading to the identification and successful prosecution of the offender The trial judge, Lord Guthrie, condemned Slater as a man who lived off the immoral earnings of prostitutes and was a jewellery thief. The police produced further evidence that

Slater (an obvious-looking German Jew) was picked out of an identity parade by a number of witnesses. The fact that he was the only Jewish and foreign looking suspect in the line up was never challenged. Slater provided two witnesses who placed him in his own home at the very time the crime was deemed to have occurred. Similarly, the prosecution failed to produce any evidence as to how Slater gained access into what was the heavily secured flat of Marion Gilchrist. The police claimed that the murder weapon was the hammer that had been found in his possession on his arrest in America. No mention was made by witnesses who claimed to see Slater after the murder, of him carrying or having in his possession a hammer. Then there was the opinion of Dr Adams, the first physician on the scene, who had declared the murder weapon was a chair; yet this evidence and his professional opinion regarding the weapon of murder was never called. Rarely has such a one sided murder trial taken place on such flimsy evidence. The police never interviewed nor investigated any other course of enquiry other than a 'suspicious man' theory. The victim's family or close friends were not interviewed, the entire focus of the investigation and subsequent trial was on Oscar Slater and fitting the acts around him.

Incredibly, nine of the jury found in favour of the prosecution, five others found the case not proven. The balance swayed in favour of the prosecution and Oscar Slater was deemed guilty of murder and so was sentenced to death by Lord Guthrie. The intrigue of this case doesn't end there, as just two days prior his execution the sentence of death was reprieved, changed to life imprisonment and hard labour. No explanation for the reprieve was ever received by Slater.

The case was taken up by fiction writer and pseudo detective Sir Arthur Conan Doyle who researched and investigated it with his best Sherlock Holmes techniques and style. Conan Doyle believed that the supposed murder weapon was far too flimsy to have been used as a powerful bludgeoning tool; furthermore, it was difficult to conceal and would be readily seen by the witnesses who sighted Slater after the crime. The one contradiction to this would be if Slater had hidden or concealed the weapon after the crime, then recovered it later

Oscar Salter in court.

when the scene was safe. Conan Doyle also believed Slater to be innocent of this crime, albeit he conceded that he was not an altogether nice person. He concluded that Marion Gilchrist must have known her attacker and allowed him or her access into her flat. He was heavily critical of the police and the manner in which they carried out their initial investigations, including the search of the murder scene and flat.

There can be little doubt too that the relatives of Marion Gilchrist were well connected and had powerful friends in high places. The evidence pointing to Slater's guilt was virtually non-existent. Many people, including Conan Doyle, formed the view that he had been fingered as suspect number one simply because the murder had to be pinned on somebody. Relentless in his efforts to prove Slater's innocence, Conan Doyle persisted his campaign of injustice over the years, submitting letters about the case to newspapers, contacts in the government and various appeals. In 1927, the Glasgow journalist, William Park, had a book upon the case published, *The Truth About Oscar Slater.* The work reviewed the entire case and arrived at the same conclusion that Conan Doyle did several years earlier, that Marion Gilchrist was likely to have known her killer and had invited him into her home. William Park further speculated that Marion Gilchrist may have initially argued with her killer, perhaps over a document that she possessed, more than likely her will. This argument had turned nasty resulting in her death. He also concluded that the murder weapon was the chair identified as such by Dr Adams. There can be little in the way of doubt that Park believed the killer to be a relative of Marion Gilchrist, angered by the revised will, and fear of libel prevented him from naming his suspect who was in his opinion the victim's nephew.

All of a sudden, the case of Oscar Slater was again big news, the book had nudged people's memories. Fresh information came to light as witnesses began to relate evidence that went unheeded at the original trial. Evidence which showed how the police brow beat by continual referrals to the £200 reward that witnesses would receive if the case was proven against Slater, into stating that he was the man seen in the vicinity of the crime. A grocer by the name of MacBrayne confirmed Slater's alibi, saying he had seen Slater on his own doorstep at the time the crime was alleged to have occurred, saying he had been smoking and seemed composed and calm, not acting as though he had just bludgeoned someone to death.

Mary Barrowman and Nellie Lambie were traced and now had to admit that they had been bribed by police to falsely identify Slater. A detective called Trench revealed that from the outset he had never believed Nellie's identification of the suspect. His honesty was his downfall as he was persecuted by his fellow police officers. Senior officers used this information against Trench and subsequently carried out an internal investigation into the facts surrounding the officer's statement to the press. He was charged with concealment of evidence and all but blamed for misguiding fellow investigating officers and causing further and wrongful investigations on an innocent man. It was a case of making him a scapegoat and a cover up of major proportions. As a result of his honesty, Trench was hounded out of the police force.

Finally, in November 1927, the newly constituted Scottish Court of Criminal Appeal pardoned Oscar Slater on the grounds that the original judge had misdirected the jury. The

Sir Arthur Conan Doyle.

Secretary of State for Scotland issued the following statement: 'Oscar Slater has now completed more than eighteen and a half years of his life sentence, and I have felt justified in deciding to authorize his release on license as soon as suitable arrangements can be made.' It was over, Oscar Slater was released.

The matter did not end there. Conan Doyle persevered with his crusade to clear Slater as his release from prison was not an official pardon, it did not exonerate him. As a result of high profile pressure, the case was reopened and once again tried, resulting in Oscar Slater being cleared of all charges against him and he was awarded compensation to the sum of £6,000.

Since then a variety of theories have been advanced by authors and amateur detectives, many of them naming individual persons, but few of their arguments are convincing. However, there are a facts that we know and others that we can reasonably assume. It is without doubt one of the most intriguing cases in Scotland's criminal history. The author is in the process of concluding twelve months serious research into the case, having reviewed and reassessed all the official and unofficial statements and evidence that exists. The result will hopefully be produced in a full-length book dedicated wholly to the crime.

CHAPTER 7

The Cost of Cheap Sex: James Rollin & Albert Fraser

1920

Prostitution, as it is often said, is the oldest profession on earth. These days, there is a new breed of male prostitutes hitting the streets of cities and towns all over the world. To sell sexual favours at an agreed rate to a paying customer is generally borne out of simple economics; it pays the rent or covers the bills. For those who believe it is only a certain class of people who frequent such a world, think again, some of the world's business executives and high profile people from the arts and culture are regular clients in the often hidden world where sex, covering every fetish, is catered for and is for sale.

In London's East End, Jack the Ripper preyed on prostitutes (or 'unfortunates' as they were also termed by Victorian society) and undoubtedly raised the profile of the profession. Much later, in late 1970s West Yorkshire, the demented serial killer Peter Sutcliffe selected the seedier side of Leeds life in order to satiate his lust for killing. Then the Leeds street girls were more naive and became easy targets for a predator such as Sutcliffe whose delusions and perverse sexual desire caused him to randomly pick on any woman who he spotted on her own, thus causing a state of terror that was not only confined to Yorkshire but spread throughout the north of England. Many women wouldn't go out alone after dark. It is no wonder then that society in general associates prostitution with human depravity, drugs and alcohol abuse; and the more gruseome side of life, including murder.

As time progressed, prostitution became big business, often acting as a front for more sinister underworld activities, the more astute criminals aware of the revenue that could be raised by managing street girls. The women or young girls who generally participated in such activity were usually in a desperate state, all with differing, desperate needs. This neediness made them vulnerable to criminals who would prey on such weakness and effectively become their manager, providing them with a pitch from which they could sell their wares and handling the cash for them, paying back a small percentage to the working girl. Today such people are regarded and are better known as 'pimps'. They are often despised and regarded as 'trash' by the more hardened members of the criminal fraternity, since in the majority of instances they rule their employees, the prostitutes, by threat and fear of physical harm.

It was just after 7.00 pm on the evening of 3 February 1920 when thirty-five-year- old Henry Senior left his home at 50 Robson Street in Govanhill, on Glasgow's south side, which he shared with his mother and brother, Henry, who had recently been discharged from the army. Henry was off out for a night on the tiles in the city centre. Before he left the house, his mother had warned him about carrying too much money; astutely she had seen him slip £10 into his coat pocket, a fair amount back then, a sum of money that would unfortunately attract the wrong kind of attention. Henry's mother was worried that her son would be attacked and robbed and urged him not to take that amount with him. To put his mother's mind at rest, he left the £10 note at home and instead went out with a more sensible amount of about £2.

Making his way from Robson Street in the direction of central Glasgow, Henry walked briskly along Hope Street, close to Argyle Street, when a young woman approached him. Henry wasn't slow on the uptake, he knew she was likely to be a prostitute. This girl didn't look like the usual sort of prostitute, this one was very pretty and had an innocence about her that greatly attracted him. Many of the older street women he had seen were very often hard-faced lasses who looked a bit worn, not very pretty. The attractive twenty-year-old woman introduced herself as Helen White, also known to her punters as Helen Keenan; dependent upon her mood and the look of the client, she would change her name to suit.

The couple stood and chatted for a while, before Helen asked Henry if he fancied going to Queens Park where they could get to know one another a bit better. Henry Senior glanced at his watch, it was still early and there would be time for a drink later, so this offer was too good to turn down. He agreed to go with the young woman. Queens Park recreation ground was synonymous with problems, older residents calling it a den of iniquity. Few sensible folk would go there after dark. A few years earlier, a vicious murder had taken place in the park, a man, rumoured to be on the prowl for cheap sex had met an untimely end and, for his sins, was beaten to death. Not that such matters were on Henry's mind, he was focused on one thing, sex.

The couple boarded a tram in Glassford Street bound for Mount Florida. He could never have known that his every move was being closely monitored by James Rollin and Albert Fraser, Helen White's pimps. They had instructed the woman to go out and find a punter for them to rob, and that punter turned out to be Henry Senior. Henry and Helen alighted the tram and made their way into the recreation ground via a fence that ran alongside the railway. There, they sat down on the grass and began to make small talk. Without warning, Henry saw two men (Rollins and Fraser) approaching. They had a look about them that made him feel uncomfortable. In a split second he also noticed that Helen was acknowledging the men and had got to her feet.

Albert Fraser pulled a revolver from his pocket and pointed in menacingly at Henry Senior. James Rollins meanwhile turned to Helen White and told her to beat it, which she did, but only moved a few yards, watching the attack from behind the fence. Senior was not about to go down without a fight and, jumping to his feet, desperately tried to resist the overpowering force of his two assailants, but was soon overcome and had his arms pinned behind his back as Fraser pistol whipped him about the face and head. Within seconds, Henry Senior was dead, the injuries caused by the butt of the revolver smashing his skull open. He dropped to the floor, motionless. Witnessing the attack, Helen White let out a scream and asked the two men not to be so hard on him which saw them do the contrary, and they continually kicked at the head and body of their victim. It made little matter, Henry Senior was in all probability dead. Helen fled the scene. The two men then took everything that Senior had with him, his boots, his overcoat and of course, his money, which was shared equally between them. They then dragged his body through some rough grass and and hid it under some nearby bushes where they left it and calmly walked away from the scene, Rollins carrying the overcoat and Fraser with each of Senior's two boot sticking out of his coat pockets. The two men were soon clear of the murder scene, boarding a tram in Langside Road that would take them back into the city where they could enjoy a drink.

It was around 11.15 pm that same evening, when the two killers again met with Helen White, she was back in her own territory, Hope Street. Helen White was mortified by what she had witnessed that evening. However, that did not stop her from going with the men to the house where Fraser lodged where they were joined by another prostitute, Elizabeth Stewart, who was often seen in company with James Rollins. For the remainder of that evening the group could think of just one thing, how they were going to escape justice. Fraser realised that there was a chance that matters would get too hot for them in Glasgow and that it would be better to flee not only the city, but the country, at least until the dust settled. He knew of a comfortable cave where they could hide out for a few days, it was by Belfast Lough in Ireland. The group all agreed and later that evening they pawned the dead man's boots, making 17s 6d, while another 8s 6d was raised by pawning the overcoat. The group then left Glasgow behind and caught the first available steamer to Belfast.

The following day two schoolboys playing in the park saw a pair of feet sticking out from behind a bush close ot the railways line. Taking a closer look they found the final remains of Henry Senior. They both rushed to alert the police. Within an hour, Assistant Chief Constable Mennie had been on scene and informed all present that he would be leading the enquiry, accompanied by Detective Chief Inspector Keith and Detective Inspector Noble. Finding clues and witnesses didn't prove too cumbersome a task. For a start, the dead man had no boots on, meaning his attacker(s) may have left the scene carrying them. The body was positively identifed by the brother of Henry Senior, who also recognised the clothes and, later, once they were retrieved, the boots and overcoat.

The local press were quickly onto the case and proved themselves to be more than useful allies, acting as formal communicators between the investigating authorities and the public criminal underworld. They requested witnesses or anyone with any knowledge of the crime or the circumstances leading up to it to come forward. Before long a witness appeared and informed the police that he had travelled on the same tram as two suspicious men, one carrying an overcoat, the other with a pair of boots sticking out of his coat pockets. It was made clear that the two men alighted the tram near Gordon Street. The pawnbroker came forward and provided further descriptions of the two men who had traded the boots and overcoat in his premises. The description matched exactly with that provided by the earlier witness.

The police search and enquiries took them onto the mean street where prostitutes patrolled more frequently than any uniformed cop. Every man and associate of the profession was spoken to, the description read out to those unable to decipher words. Soon the investigation had names for their suspects, two ponces or pimps known as James Rollins and Albert Fraser, last known to have been seen accompanied by their two prostitutes (White and Stewart). Another informant came forward and told the police that Fraser often spoke of how – if he should ever find himself wanted by the Glasgow cops – he would lie low in a cave by Belfast Lough. The press coverage had an adverse effect on the community as many people of both sexes became scared to go out into the south side unless they desperately needed to do so. The local night time economy was beginning to suffer, therefore it was in everyone's best interest that the police caught the killer or killers and locked them away.

The amount and quality of the evidence coming into the investigation was exceptional as criminals with a vested interest in the local community came forward with masses of information. Within a couple of days of the murder taking place, the cops had a complete picture of the route taken by the group after they left the park and went to a hotel, then a bar, and finally took the Belfast Boat Train at Glasgow Central Station. On 7 February 1920, the police, represented by Detective Chief Inspector Keith and Detective Inspector Noble left Glasgow and sailed for Belfast. Their principle quarry were twenty-two-year-old James Rollins and twenty-four-year old Albert Fraser and their respective partners (White and Stewart). On arrival in Belfast, the two Glasgow cops liaised with their Royal Irish Constabulary counterparts and pretty soon a body of police officers made their way to Belfast Lough. A thorough search of the entire Lough area was carried out, and the cave quickly identifed. A precision entry into the mouth of the cave caught the two male members of the gang off guard, and they were each placed under arrest on suspicion of the murder of Henry Senior. Taken back to a local police station, they were charged then conveyed back to Glasgow for further interview.

Both of the accused refused to cooperate with the police questioning, and denied everything put to them, even to the extent that they knew the two prostitutes in question. A thorough search of their persons was carried out. Fraser was found to have a large bloodstain on the cuff of his shirt and jacket, which he could not account for; but this wasn't sufficient in the way of evidence to prove the men's guilt. A search of Rollins' pockets provided the lucky break every police investigation needs. In one was a piece of paper bearing an address and the names of Helen White and Elizabeth Stewart. Uniformed officers were sent out and shortly after returned with the two wanted women.

The women were clearly in a state of terror, particularly Helen who blurted out the entire story and how horrified she had been. She claimed that since the murder she had not slept a wink, constantly worrying and was wracked by guilt. The police played their master card and had soon convinced both women to turn King's Evidence and testify against their pimps. Helen White in particular was to be the leading witness in the case of the prosecution.

At the trial, which took place on 4 May 1920 at the High Court, Glasgow, the sickening tale of how the two pimps abused the two prostitutes, using them as bait to attract a certain kind of man and lead him to Queens Park recreation ground where they (Rollins and Fraser) would lay in wait and carry out robberies. Helen spoke in some detail of how she accosted the smartly dressed Henry Senior in Hope Street, at the pimps request. In the park they couple had been seated when Rollins charged out of some nearby bushes, yelling at Henry and asking 'what the fuck he was doing?' She explained how Henry had replied in a calm manner, that he was simply walking his girl and what was wrong with that. Upon which Fraser emerged from the bushes and the two men began to grapple with Henry Senior, smashing his face until it was little more than a blood-covered mass of pulp.

The trial lasted two days and during cross-examination the two female witnesses (White and Stewart) were forced to reveal how they had been party to several similar attacks that had not resulted in murder, but were more akin to blackmail as the victims, many of whom were 'allegedly' happily married men would hand over cash in order to buy the assailant's silence. Despite the participation in these crimes, the jury found the evidence provided by the two prostitutes to be compelling and wholly believable. After retiring from the court to assess the evidence, the jury returned after just twenty minutes with a unanimous 'guilty' verdict against both defendents (Rollins and Fraser). The trial judge, Lord Justice Sands, informed the two men that he had little sympathy for them and that their cowardly crime deserved the ultimate punishment. His clerk moved forward to place the black cap on his lordship's head as he sentenced both men to hang.

So it was that at 8.00 am on the morning of 26 May 1920, James Rollins and Albert Fraser were executed by hangman John Ellis, at Duke Street Prison. This, as it so happened, was the last double hanging that took place at the prison. Outside the gaol walls a few hundred dispassionate folk had gathered,

John Ellis the hangman.

none seeming to hold any sympathy for the either of the convicted felons. Once the formal notice that the execution had been carried out was posted on the prison doors, the crowd quickly dissipated without a murmur of objection.

Duke Street prison, scene of execution.

Murdered in the Name of Politics

1921

It is often said that the greatest cause of human tragedy is either politics or religion. Far too many lives have been lost over the years through warfare, a situation which never seems to ease in a global sense. A state of guerilla warfare between the armed forces of Great Britain and the Irish (mainly since the Republic of Ireland set up its own parliament in 1919) has existed. The year 1921 wasn't a particularly good one when it comes to political murder, in Ireland the vicious killing of two innocent young men, Patrick and Daniel Duffin in their home, allegedly by members of the Royal Irish Constabulary had caused great public outrage. It was a period when shocking violence was a regular occurrence. Glasgow, during this same era, was a city with many Irish sympathisers, many of whom would provide a safe house, a bolthole, for persons associated with or who were sympathisers to the hostilities. As a result the Glasgow police were kept bust trying to track down and identiy al such activities and persons, and as such were called upon to search homes or make arrests of wanted persons.

One such man was Frank J Carty, alias Somers, who was, allegedly, a commandant in the Irish Republican Army (IRA). Carty was wanted by the Irish authorities for prison breaking and for the theft of a firearm, a service revolver. He was highly repescted amongst his peers and was regarded as something of a martyr to the cause. On 28 April 1921, Carty was arrested by Glasgow police, his detention being widely reported in the press and on the street. Whilst this was something of a kudos for Glasgow police, it also provided unwanted attention and rumours soon began to surface that Carty would be the subject of a prison break.

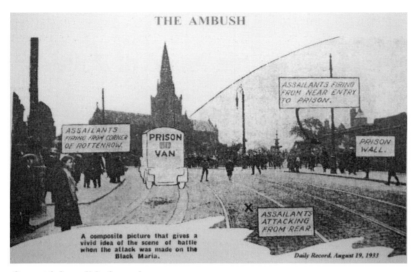

Scene of the political murder.

In an effort to deal with the security situation as reasonably as possible, Carty was escorted in the black maria, to and from prison, through the city and to the Central police court in St Andrews Square, by a posse of police officers, some armed. On his second such appearance at the court on Wednesday the 4th of May, he was again remanded in custody, this time for four days at Duke Street prison. The transfer of the prisoner on this specific day had alerted extra security measures, it wasn't as though the journey was any different, it was the same route this same vehicle would make throughout the majority of its working life. It was the securty threat that Carty posed. The black maria contained two prosiners that day, Carty and one other prisoner, both men were secured in the separate metal compartments (dog boxes) that are to be found within almost all prisoner escort vehicles. Joining the prisoners inside the vehicle was Constables George Bernard and David Brown. At the front of the vehicle was Constable Thomas Ross who was the driver and beside him sat Inspector Robert Johnston, Detective Sergeant George Stirton, and Detective constable Murdoch MacDonald, the latter two officer being armed with service style revolvers.

It was shortly after midday when the Black Maria prison van made its way up the hill that was High Street, all was quiet, the rumours of the springing of heir prisoner seemed to have no credence as Constable Tom Ross slowed the vehicle down to manouevre from High Street into Cathedral Square opposite the water-pumping station. Then it happened...all hell broke loose.

According to witesses and the police officers themselves, three individual groups of men totalling around thirty in all, suddenly came at the now stationary polie vehicle from all directions. In an attempt to flea the scene, Ross managed to keep the van moving and turned into Cathedral Square where the prison wall runs along one side. Suddenly, several shots were fired at the police vehicle, originally from the direction of the corner of Rottenrow. Within moments, the sound of gun fire filled the air, innocent people on the streets ran for cover, screaming and forcing their way into anywhere that would afford sanctuary from the hail of bullts that was now showering the police vehicle. In a desperate attempt ot defend themselves, the police fired back at the mob, Detective Sergeant Stirton shooting through the windscreen on the van and out onto the street. Suddenly, with the windscreen shattered, the occupants sat in the front of the van were left exposed and vulnerable. Stirton yelled out instructions, telling the unarmed Inspector Johnston to take cover and to run for his life. Johnston, in an effort to get out of the front of the vehicle was stepping down out of the front cab when he was fatally struck twice by bullets fired by the marauding mob. His now limp body fell out of the van and spilled out onto the street below, his face bloodied and now without emotion. He was dead.

There was no time for the remaining officers to think about the state of the Inspector, the attack continued as the vehicle was now surrounded. Many of the mob had gathered at the rear of the vehicle, and were trying to force open the locked and secured rear doors in an attempt to free Frank Carty. Shots were fired into the lock and attempts were made to forcibly pull the doors open, they wouldn't budge. Stirton and his colleagues meanwhile were desperately trying to fend off further attack and deaths. In the volley of gunshots that followed, Storton was struck on the wrist, shattering the bone, but still he refused to concede and bravely fought on. Detective Constable MacDonald was now the only armed police offer who was without injury who could return fire with an accuracy, however, such was the quantity of bullets flying around that he was forced to defend his position using the van as cover. In the drivers seat, Tom Ross hit the floor, feigning death in an attempt to save his own life, his priority was to get the Black Maria to the prison, an impossible task while all the gunfire was taking place. Suddenly a man, one of the attackers tried to remove Ross from the van, defiantly, the unarmed officer slugged it out fist to fist with a number of his attackers, temporarily repelling them.

Without warning, all the action tiurned to the rear of the vehicle where the majority of the angry mob had now congregated, shots were being fired into the side walls of the van, as the gathered throung in depseration tried anything and everything to release their man. Stirton recklessly, although some may may save bravely, made his way to the rear of the van and confronted the mob, raising his revolver and pointing at the men closest to the rear doors of the vehicle threatened to fire. There was an errie silence before the groups of men suddenly opted to flea the scene, scattering in all directions and disappearing into the surrounding streets and alleys as quickly as they had appeared. Stirton tried to puruse some of them, he was haemorrhaging much blood and elected to return to check on Inspector Johnston.

It was a scene of absolute carnage, Johnston lay on the floor motionless, his face splattered by his own crimson red blood. Support police officers quickly arrived on the scene and took both Johnston and Stirton to the Royal Infirmary, where Johnston was subsequently anounced as dead. To his credit, Constable Ross somehow managed to get the bullet-riddled Black Maria started and drove it into Duke Street Prison. Within this sanctuary, the authorities tried toopen the rear doors but found them jammed shut. The lock couldn't be forced and it took over three hours before it could be opened and the prisoners and their police escorts clambered out, weeping and sobbing hysterically through fear.

Medals of decoration for George Stirton.

News of the crime swept through the streets of Glasgow far swifter than any newspaper could deliver it. Within hours, what was at first an inquisitive and sympathetic crowd attended the crime scene, however, as news spread that the police were responding to the assault by arresting any suspect in the east end who couldn't provide an alibi for their whereabouts at the time of the murder, the crowd soon turned hostile. Many arrests were made in the Gallowgate area and particular attention was made to the houses of known sympathisers, including a priest. As the crowd gathered at the scene of the murder and began to express their discontent, the police moved in using heavy handed tactics and arresting anyone and everyone voicing their concerns. Matters deteriorated. As further arrests were made throughout the day, the anger within the various communities heightened to dangerous levels. Across the east end police officers were chased by gangs of men, property looted and thousands of pounds worth of damage caused by rioters. Over forty policemen were injured or assaulted during such demonstrations. The Central police court was bursting with prisoners the following morning, as twenty persons (14 men and 6 women) appeared there, charged with: having discharged loaded firearms while attempting to rescue a prisoner, killed Inspector Johnston, wounded Detective Sergeant Stirton. All were remanded in custodt for forty eight hours while investigations continued. Within a week this figure rose to thirty four persons in custody. To prevent further complications from within prison, Frank Carty was secretly removed from Glasgow and taken to Dublin where he was handed over to the Irish authorities. During the continuing police enquiries, Detective Lieutenant John Forbes visited 74 Abercormbie Street and during the ensuing search of the property unveiled the largest haul of ammunition and explosives ever found in Glasgow. It consisted of thirty-five revolvers, six hand grenades, a bomb, several pounds of gelegnite, detonators, eight bags of percussion caps, fuse wire, 955 rounds of rifle and revlover ammunition, magazines and holsters. Finally, just thirteen prisoners were brought to trial at Edinburgh, each charged with the aforestated offences, plus an addiitonal one of conspiracy. Detective Sergeant Stirton and positively identified nine of the assailents and provided graphc detail of how the men had approached the police vehicle, lined up along the pavement and rested their revolvers on their left arms before firing into the prisoner escort vehicle. His evidence was brought into doubt by the defence team, who accused him of panicvking and opening fire first, they followed this assertion (which was refused by the police hero) by asking how he was capable of making positive prisoner identification during such a frantic attack. He stuck to his evidence and never once faltered while giving evidence. Detective Constable MacDonald did likewise, he identified six of the prisoners. Once again the accurasy of his testimony was queried. The trial lasted a full eleven days as the defence began to dissolve the prosecution case, providing alibi's for each of the defendents, and accusing the police of showing witnesses images of the accused in order that they should positively identify them in court. The entire case hinged on how much the jury trusted or believed police evidence, evidence that had come from the undoubted heroes of the three minute attack. It mattered little. Each of the accused was to walk free from the court, six of them were found 'not guilty' by the jury of seven men and eight women, the cases against the remaining seven prisoners were found 'not proven.' It was a devastating blow for the police, one of their officers had been murdered, unarmed and offering no threat whatsoever, he had been slain on the street in cold blood. The jury had ignored that and no one was ever brought to justice for the murder. Some claim that the jury themselves were in fear of physical reprisals, hence their verdict. Whatever the case, the memory of the bravery displayed by all the officers on that fateful day in May 1921 should stand as a beacon of testimony and awareness of every police officer who dons the uniform and commits to the serious responsibility it holds.

CHAPTER 9

The Whiteinch Murder: William & Helen Harkness

1921

Today, Whiteinch is a district that lies north of the Clyde is situated between Partick and Scotstoun. An area rich in history it was an integral part of the renewed and ever growing city of Glasgow in 1921 when it fell within the Parish of Govan. Looking back on its past it is recorded that it was once called Whyt Inch (the term 'Inch' refers to a Scottish Island) an island located in the river Clyde, this was when it was shallow and flowed through the forces of nature. The island eventually disappeared when the Clyde was reduced in width and other non natural physical alterations were made to it such as dredging and narrowing, this was to compliment the expansion of ship building in the city. However, despite its physical disappearance, Whiteinch as a community and district today lives on in the west of the city and north of the river.

As a community it expanded with the industrial growth of the city and in particular that related to ship building. One of the biggest of the era being the Clydeholm shipyard, originally opened in 1855, which ran along a vast extent of the Whiteinch riverbank and was at one time owned by the Barclay Curle company. Not unnaturally, the district was very much working class and with that was poverty and deprivation. Housing conditions and human health were not always good. As something of a natural juxtaposition to the often squalid living and social conditions of the environment was Fossil Grove in the beautiful Victoria Park. There eleven fossil trees, Lepidodendron ("Giant club moss") were originally uncovered by removal of rock in 1887. The old quarry which existed there was essentially being landscaped during the creation of Victoria Park. The fossilised remains of the ancient forest are believed to be around 330 million years old and have been preserved and protected by the erection of a building around them. Areas of such natural beauty within the inner city conurbation are rare anywhere across the world, making Whiteinch unique and very special.

William Harkness cared little about areas of natural beauty that existed within the district of Whiteinch, even though it was less than one hundred yards from his home. At 31 years of age he was a much more mercenary and self centred character, a driller his profession didn't provide much in the way of financial income to the home he shared with 28 year old Helen M'Leary or Harkness, the couple resided at 67 George Street (later known as Medwyn Street), Whiteinch. George street was a busy thoroughfare and had within its confines a public swimming baths, schools and a number of religious establishments. It was also home to thousands of people, mainly in rented rooms. In 1921 it is fair to say that it was at the centre of much of the social activity within the district, the housing however, was of poor quality and more importantly grossly overcrowded.

Crowds flock to scene of the murder.

On the 31 October 1921, George Street became the focus of a good deal of unwanted attention when a sickening and quite unnecessary murder occurred at number 67, home of William and Helen Harkness. Their victim was a young 14 year old jewish girl, a mere child whose only crime was being in the wrong place at the wrong time. Elizabeth Benjamin who lived at 1 North Elgin Street, Clydebank, was well known and respected in the district, as a sensible hard working young girl. On the day in question she had called at Harkness home to collect some outstanding monies the couple owed, a debt. Whilst there was plenty of people who had little good to say about either William or Helen Harkness, there were those who believed that Helen was suppressed by her overpowering husband, bullied and intimidated into doing as he demanded.

On calling at the Harkness home, Elizabeth Benjamin went missing; she was never again seen alive. A search for the young girl commenced, and all the homes she was due to visit were called upon, with the exception of the Harkness home all were helpful and offered to assist in the search for the mysterious disappearance of the young girl. Within hours a search was carried out at number 67 George Street by the authorities. It was clear from the outset that the Harkness's were not going to cooperate with the police. However, they had little choice but to allow access to the search party into their home. The couple were defensive and tried to persuade the unwanted visitors to look in areas dictated by them. As the search continued blood stain and smears were found on the wallpaper within the house, William Harkness claimed that the smears had come from him when he had suffered a cut. Further blood stains were found on the plaster, these seemed reasonably fresh. Eventually as the search moved into the back yard of the property and in particular the wash house. There the dead body of the missing child was found, she had been brutally attacked.

Her hands had been tied behind her head by a rope that was fastened round the wrists, and there was a severe wound to her blood covered head. Blood was smeared onto a water boiler which stood next to the body and other areas. An attempt to force the body behind the boiler and to hide it had been made.

Further examination of the remains revealed that a cotton handkerchief had been forced into the girls mouth and down her throat.

William and Helen Harkness were at once arrested and taken away for police questioning. Meanwhile in George Street an excitable and noisy crowd of around 500 local folk gathered to look at the murder scene and to witness the removal of the dead girl. Ghoulish souvenir hunters managed to remove objects within the house and a lynch mob was keen to pursue their own punishment on the couple. The police managed to quell the anger and assured the gathered throng that justice would be done.

The police investigation was fairly straight forward; it was clear that she had been murdered within 67 George Street by the couple, neither of who would confess to the crime, therefore both were remanded in custody. The couple appeared before Police Judge Drummond, at Partick Police Court, confirmed their identities and their home address, Helen Harkness pleaded for mercy and her innocence. Her cries of desperation had no effect as the couple were remanded for 48 hours for inquiries to continue. The press of the day recorded a description of the two persons in detention.

'The man, who at the pleading diet ten days ago had been unshaven, and was wearing a muffler, looked considerably brighter on that occasion. He seemed to be about thirty years of age, and was wearing a soft collar and black tie, with a dark suit. His wife also appeared respectably dressed in a navy blue coat and hat. She appeared, if anything, to be younger than her husband.'

After a thorough and lengthy investigation the case was eventually tried at Glasgow High Court on the 30th January, 1922. Seldom can their have been a more comprehensive criminal investigation with an overwhelming number of witnesses, seventy for the crown, including neighbours and people who knew the Harkness couple and claimed William to be a devious and often viscously spoken man with a propensity for violence. Prior to the crime he had been overheard discussing easy ways to come into money with a number of 'known' undesirables. Helen meanwhile was also described as

Trial of William and Helen Harkness.

a victim of her husbands behaviour, many believed that she was incapable of harming anyone. She possessed a foul mouth and could give a tongue lashing to those who crossed her, but violent she was not. The crown produced eleven physical exhibits these included microscopic slides showing smears taken from stains on a washing house-boiler, numerous parts of the boiler, and pieces of wallpaper and plaster that were also blood stained.

The prosecution revealed that the sole motive for the crime had been theft, as two pounds was missing from Elizabeth Benjamin's purse. William Harkness was identified as being the assailant and had overpowered the girl who had fought back, only to be beaten about the head with a reamer (a cone-shaped cutting tool used to convert cylindrical mortises into a cone-like configuration) or other similar blunt instrument. He had then tied her hands behind her head, beaten and abused her and robbed her of the two pounds. In an attempt to silence the girls screams for help during the attack, he had forced a handkerchief into her throat, whereby she suffocated. He then tried to hide the body behind the water boiler.

The defence could offer nothing in the way of evidence to disprove the allegations

And at 2.53 p.m. on the 31st of January 1922, the jury, having heard all the details of the crime, retired from the court to deliberate on their verdict. They returned some 26 minutes later at 3.19 p.m. The verdict was a unanimous one, both of the accused were guilty of murder. The jury did however, make a strong recommendation for mercy on behalf of Helen Harkness who they felt was a forced accomplice. Both William and Helen Harkness were sentenced to death though Helen's sentence was, on 18 February 1922 subsequently commuted to penal servitude for life.

William Harkness was given no such reprieve and was hanged by on 21st February 1922 in Duke Street Prison, Glasgow. He went to his death in a cold and calculated manner, his arms pinioned and the white cap draped over his head to hide the facial disfiguration caused during the execution. Ellis was the executioner, he was assisted by Willis.

Two lives lost and many others destroyed for the sake of just two pounds, the crime of William and Helen Harkness cast a dark shadow over Whiteinch for many years. The killers name was only used in an insulting manner by locals who occasionally referred to the crime. Whether Helen deserved to be reprieved or not is quite another matter, many living in the district believed that justice was done, others meanwhile felt that she had escaped reasonable punishment. No matter what, nothing could ever bring back the unfortunate Elizabeth Benjamin, an innocent child robbed not only of money but of her life and all that offered her.

CHAPTER 10

The Go-Cart Tragedy: Susan Newell

1923

The murder of an innocent child quite properly tends to draw out a mass of public hysteria and emotional sympathy for family and relatives. It also brings into question what could have been done to prevent such an awful act from occurring in the first place. One such crime occurred in the rented rooms of a tiny terraced house at number 2 Newlands Street, Coatbridge. Little Johnny Johnston, aged just thirteen years, from 23 Whifflett Street, Coatbridge, met with a tragic and sad end to his life for the sake of 9d (4p). Afterwards, his mortal remains were shown anything but respect by the perpetrator of this malicious act, namely, one Susan Newell.

Susan Newell was born in 1893 and was one of thirteen children. She was described as hailing from the 'tinker class'. She lived a miserable existence, raised amidst a community where little in the way of morals or principles existed. Susan and her peers grew up believing that in life other people's property could be yours. If you wanted something and it didn't belong to you, you would take it by whatever means were available. Where human life was concerned, people were expendable, she had witnessed first hand and learned the ways of the streets where thuggery and street theft was an everyday activity, causing harm to another human being acceptable to her kind and life was in effect cheap. It was an existence of monotonous poverty and deprivation, where only the strongest survived. With several failed relationships behind her, including a marriage from which she had one child, a girl called Janet, who kept the surname (McLeod) from the failed relationship.

By 1923, Susan had married again, to John Newell, and was renting rooms at 2 Newlands Street, Coatbridge. Janet was now eight and rarely left her mother's side, refusing to afford any parental status or to acknowledge John Newell as a father figure whatsoever. In essence, the child was in her mother's image, taking all she could from John Newell and giving nothing, not one ounce of respect in return. Not that respect should be free, nor that John Newell deserved it, he was hardly a role model parent himself. For a start, he enjoyed a drink and had a bit of a reputation with the women in the district and around Glasgow. He was though, a good provider and worked hard to bring in funds to keep a roof over his family, put food on the table and, importantly to him, beer in his belly. Recently he had been laid off from his regular employment as a tube worker, a situation which had hardly helped the family unity. It's fair to say that couple had a tempestuous relationship in which John generally came off worst. Susan was a little too handy with her fists or anything that would serve as a weapon against her husband.

On Tuesday 19 June, a quarrel between the pair had erupted, resulting in Susan attacking John and causing cutting and brusing to his face. Such was John Newell's distress at this situation, he reported the assault to the police. However, as both were well known for their drunken brawls locally, no immediate action was taken. The following day she continued with her vitriolic manners and severely beat him yet again, causing him to move out. The couple's landlady, Mrs Annie Young, on hearing yet another fracas from within the rooms, gave them both notice to leave the premises as soon as possible.

John Newell was in a mess, his marriage was over and to further compound his miserable situation his brother had died resulting in him attending the funeral, visting his father and staying overnight in a Parkhead lodging house. He once again sought sollace through alcohol and was out with another brother, David, when an incensed Susan Newell hunted him down. Confronting him in the street, she ordered him to go back home to Newlands Street. John refused, reaffirming the fact that their relationship was over, something she had constantly requested of him on more than one ocassion during their marriage of just over seven months. Susan would have none of it, and lunged at her husband, head butting him in the face and damaging his nose. Before leaving him laid in the street she further threatened him, with an intent to have him locked up for wife-desertion. He later returned to his lodging house and then visited a music hall in the East End where he was regularly undercharged by a barman for beer. After this he visited his sister's home. There he confessed to being worried by the threats his wife had made. Sensibly, the sister reassured him that as he was regularly beaten by his wife, often in front of witnesses, he had an alibi for leaving her, his personal safety. Later that evening, John Newell visited a police station, and asked there if he was wanted for wife-desertion. He was told that he was not. The following day, 21 June 1923, he travelled to Haddington, East Lothian in search of work. These are the known facts about the Newells and provide the backdrop to one of the most despicable crimes of the era.

In the early evening of 20 June 1923, Johnny Johnston was out helping his pal deliver and sell newspapers. He had in his pocket 9d, acquired from the evening sales of newspaper. A bright and personable young boy, he was regarded as a happy young man who always had a smile on his face. The Newells' landlady, Mrs Annie Young, saw the young man go to the Newells' door at around 6.55 pm. Shortly afterwards she heard three thumps from within the rooms. She presumed the boy had left, although she had not seen him do so, nor had she seen John Newell at all during that entire day. The cause of the 'bump' noise heard by Mrs Young can only be guessed as being the vicious assault on young Johnny Johnston.

A short time later, Susan Newell knocked upon the door of Mrs Young's room and asked her if she had a box to pack things. Mrs Young told the woman she had nothing suitable. Later that evening Mrs Young saw Susan leave the house along with her daughter. It was clear that they were heading for the pub as she carried with her a jug into which beer could be poured and carried – not unusual practice for the Newell family who generally spent much time in drink. Number 2 Newlands Street was to be a hive of activity that evening, through to the early hours of the morning. Initially, the mother and daughter returned from the pub a few minutes later carrying the jug of beer, and remained in their rooms for only a short time before once again going out for a couple of hours. Again they returned, only for Susan to again venture out again. By now it was around 11 pm. Mrs Young finally heard her return and ultimately settle down for the night, at some time after 2am. The following morning, at about 8 am, Mrs Young had gone to bring in the milk, and noticed that the front door of 2 Newlands Street was open, yet inside there was no sign of Newell. It was not until later that day that she heard the news that Susan Newell and her daughter had been taken into police custody on suspicion of murder.

Inside the police station at Tobago Street, Glasgow, Susan Newell explained that she was innocent of any such crime as murder and that she too was a victim, explaining to the investigating police that her husband was a drunk and extremely violent man and how she had suffered. She claimed that during one such violent quarrel on the evening of 20 June he had struck her, an action witnessed by the young paper boy. John Newell had then took hold of the boy and throttled him to death. In fear of her own safety, Susan Newell had agreed to get rid of the body on behalf of her husband. Quite incredibly, eight-year-old Janet McLeod told the police precisely the same story, ensuring that John Newell, still in East Lothian, became principal suspect.

The local press covered the story and further revealed that John Newell was wanted by the police on suspicion of murder. Within twenty-four hours he was under lock and key. Having read and been told that he was wanted by the police, John Newell did the honourable thing and handed himself into a police station, where he at once provided himself with an alibi that virtually proved his innocence. He said he had travelled to Haddington and booked into a lodging house as he tried to find farm work. He had witnesses who would vouch for his whereabouts on the night and at the times in question. Despite this, the police, succumbing to public and media pressure had got the wanted man. The last thing they wanted was the potential public outrage that would follow if they released him without charge. John Newell was returned to Glasgow, taken to Tobago Street police station and charged with the murder.

The following day, Professor John Glaister and Dr John Anderson of the Victoria Infirmary carried out a post-mortem examination on the body of what the press referred to as the 'dead lad' at Glasgow's Central Police Mortuary. There they found that he had been beaten about the head with a blunt instrument, and strangled with such force as to dislocate the spinal column in the poor boy's neck. A search of the scene of the crime, 2 Newlands Street, revealed the probable murder weapon, or at the very least, that used in the initial assault – a substantial metal poker.

The father of the dead boy, Robert Johnston, was told of the crime. He explained to the police that on the night his lad had failed to come home, he thought that he may have gone to the cinema with some of his earnings. By the time it had got to 10.30 pm, which was generally the time when the pictures ended, he became more concerned by the non-appearance of his son. In a state of absolute panic he had scoured the streets and park areas looking for him. Unable to locate the lad, he had turned into his bed holding onto the belief that Johnny was perhaps staying out at one of his pal's homes. However, as it was so out of context with the way the boy normally acted and there was no previous history of such things taking place, he had felt extremely worried by the situation. The following day he had gone to work as usual, half expecting his son to return home that morning. It wasn't to be.

Later that morning, a uniformed police officer visited Johnston's workplace and called him out. He explained that a body had been found and early suggestions were that it was the remains of his son, Johnny. Robert Johnston was taken to Glasgow's Eastern police station, briefed on the situation and asked to compose himslef as best he could under the circumstances. He was then shown a body. A police officer asked him if he knew whose body it was. One can only imagine the utter grief that this man must have felt as he saw laying before him the beaten body of his young son. He broke down, sobbing uncontrollably, saying: 'Oh! My boy's body.' It was a testing time for the police who realised that the press would be hunting out as much information as they could about the deceased's family and of those of the persons charged. Robert Johnston meanwhile had the further gruesome task of formally identifying his son's clothing. In the interest of swift justice, both of the accused had hearings at independent courts before the official formal proceedings took place at Glasgow High Court. The actions and apparent lack of remorse displayed by Susan Newell had aroused much public angst. It is said that queues of witnesses lined up outside Tobago Street police station to provide statements regarding her movement on the night of the murder and the following morning. Whereas John Newell continued to protest his innocence, no one, it seemed, wanted to hear his alibi, thereby absolving themselves of making any decision as to his innocence prior to the trial.

By the time the trial came around, the police had gathered a wealth of evidence against Susan Newell, but little or nothing against her husband. The only damning evidence that related to him had come from the mouth of Susan Newell and her daughter. However, various witnesses had come forward to state the disdain the young girl felt towards her step-father and how she would always do exactly as her mother asked.

An entire area was gripped by the detail and the apparent veil of mystery that surrounded the case. Shortly after midnight in the morning of Tuesday, 18 September 1923, people had started to queue in the streets surrounding the court building, in the hope of getting a seat to view both the accused and to hear the sordid and sanguinary details of the crime for themselves. The court public gallery was packed when Susan Newell and husband John were brought into the dock. The accused couple appeared together, separated and flanked on either side by uniformed police officers. John Newell looked a tired and broken man, wearing a suit and clutching a flat cap in his hands. His wife was sombrely dressed in dark clothes and had the appearance of an aged and haggard woman who didn't seem to care about proceedings taking place around her. She was represented by her counsel, TA Gentles, KC, who at once lodged a special plea of insanity at the time of the murder. Whereas the counsel representing her husband, Archibald Crawford, KC, lodged a special defence of alibi. The proceedings were further delayed as Mr Gentles objected to every woman who had been selected for the jury, believing that to have a woman on the jury would damage his client's claim of innocence. The reality was that no woman or mother could ever accept or understand how another mother could commit such a heinous act on a child. Eventually, an all-male line-up was selected as the jury.

From ther outset, Susan's defence was based upon the fact that she was innocent and that her husabnd was the killer. She stuck to her original story that was first recorded by the police. Her daughter, Janet MacLeod, was asked to give evidence. The young girl told how she recalled going to Duffy's pub with her mum on the evening of the murder and being left outside. As her mum had gone inside to have a jug filled with beer, she then came out and the two returned home. Gentle probing by the advocate and counsel for the Crown, Lord Kinross, caused the question to be asked as to what she had seen in the room at 2 Newlands Street. Janet replied: 'A little wee boy dead on the couch.' Lord Kinross followed this up by asking: 'How did you know?'

The dialogue continued as follows:

Janet: 'I went over to look.'

Lord Kinross: 'Did your mother do anything?'

Janet: 'She drank the beer.'

Lord Kinross: 'Did she do anything about the boy?'

Janet: 'She was trying to get up the floor.'

Lord Kinross: 'Did she touch the boy?'

Janet: 'Yes.'

Lord Kinross: 'What did she do?'

Janet: 'She took my father's pair of drawers and put them over his face.'

After further questioning, Janet conceded that she had not seen the boy harmed, thereby negating her previous claim that she saw her step father, John Newell, kill the boy. Lord Kinross teased all the vital information from the child witness including important and damning detail about how the body of the dead boy was disposed and the circumstances leading up to the arrest of her mother. When asked by Kinross: 'What did you do with the wee laddie?' Janet replied: 'We put him in a bag. There was a bed mat in it. We went downstairs and I got toffee. There was a go-cart and I got a seat on it.'

Probing further, Kinross queried: 'When you sat in it, what did you sit on? The bundle?' To which Janet responded: 'Yes, on the wee boy.'

Gradually, every sordid detail of the morbid affair was being extracted from the witnesses. John Newell was asked to stand as information relating to his whereabouts at the time and on the night of the crime was revealed. The police supported his claim that he was elsewhere and therefore could not have taken any part in the murder. Sensationally, he was allowed to walk free from the court without further participation, the murder charge againt him dropped from the record. He looked a very relieved if not emotional man who was quite horrified by the facts of the case against his wife as they were revealed one by one. As he walked from the dock he did not look at nor speak to his wife, whereas Susan Newell fixed a cold stare twoards her husband, keeping her eyes firmly fixed upon him until he was out of her view. The atmosphere in the court house had now intensified ten fold, as Susan Newell stood alone in the dock as the sole accused; a fact that seemed to have no emotional impact on her whatsoever.

The case for the prosecution claimed that Susan Newell had invited Johnny Johnston into her rooms, asked him for a newspaper then refused to pay for it. When the child had asked for the money she struck him three times about the head with a heavy steel poker, before strangling him until he was black in the face. In an attempt to disguise her crime she had then set about trying to get rid of the body, initially by burning it but when that didn't work she tried to bury it under the floorboards of her home. Finally, with the assistance of little Janet MacLeod, she had packed the corpse into a brightly coloured blanket or quilt before putting it in a go-cart, covering it with blankets and then pushing it several miles from her home in Glasgow, with her daughter sat on top of the bundle containing the dead child.

Together the mother and daughter had got about eight miles from their home when a lorry driver gave them a lift into the city. Thomas Gibson, from Airdrie, was called to the witness box and told how he was driving his lorry on the day in question and had stopped to give Susan Newella and her daughter a lift. He helped her to lift the go-cart onto the truck. Then continued on his way further into Glasgow. It was during this journey that Newell told him that she was looking for rooms for her and her daughter. As they got to Duke Street in the city he dropped her off. As she was removing the go-cart from the lorry the bundle that was carried on it slipped, he had tried to help her get it to the ground safely, adding: 'You're in an awful hurry.' Newell turned on him and pushed him away and scoldingly telling him: 'Get on your lorry. I'll manage it myself.'

Unbeknown to Newell or Gibson as they stood there beside the lorry, they were being watched by a local resident, Helen Elliott, who was peering down on the scene from an upstairs window of her home, 602 Duke Street. Mrs Elliott was called to give evidence and aroused gasps of horror from the public gallery as she revealed what she was seen: 'I was amazed when the bundle slipped. I saw a child's foot appear from beneath the blanket. As the woman (Newell) tried to cover it in some haster, I caught sight of a head at the other end of the bundle. I could see it was a child, probably dead.'

Mrs Elliott had watched Newell move further into the close before leaving her own home to go in search of a policeman which she found nearby and told of what she had witnessed. Susan Newell had just dumped the body in the close of the tenement at 650 Duke Street, when Constable Thomas McGennet approached her. In a state of blind panic Newell tried to climb a wall in an attempt to escape. The constable was too quick for her and within seconds had her apprehended, though she did put up a struggle and had tried to hit the officer several times during her arrest.

Her counsel, TA Gentles KC, suggested that his client had been insane at the time of the crime, caused through years of abuse. The defence produced expert witnesses who not only disagreed with this claim, but disproved it. The trial had lasted just two days yet there seemed little doubt that Susan Newell was the killer of the young paper boy, a fact supported by the jury who took just thirty-seven minutes to reach their 'guilty' verdict. Susan Newell stared with cold empty eyes and almost in contempt as the judge ignored the recommendation for mercy and reached for the black cap, revealing that Susan Newell would be exectued on 10 October 1923 at Duke Street Prison. An appeal against the judgment was lodged but formally rejected.

There are various tales as to how she met her end, one being that she refused the traditional white hood as she climbed on the gallows. Another version claims that she met her death with defiance and that just seconds before the trap door opened, she managed to break a hand free from her tethers and immediately ripped off the white hood, and staring into the faces of her executioners screamed out: 'Don't put that thing over me.' Whatever the situation, hangman John Ellis dispatched Newell from this earth on Wednesday 10 October 1923, with hardly a resident of Glasgow caring or shedding a tear, save perhaps her young daughter who was taken into care of the authorities. Susan Newell was the last woman to be executed in Scotland. Her reputation as a loathsome, uncaring creature forever etched in history by virtue of the callous crime she committed. It is curious to note that where she dumped the body of her victim was within close proximity of Duke Street prison where she met her fate. Right up to her death, she continued to deny that she was the killer, a somewhat futile plea that fell on the deaf ears of an entire nation.

CHAPTER 11

The Fiend of the Gorbals: Patrick Carraher

1938

Over the years, Scotland and in particular Glasgow, has had its fair share of 'hard men' who gained their reputation as tough no nonsense individuals who tended to get their own way. Unfairly, not all of them were of the criminal fraternity as they had no intention of making any personal gain from their activity, in fact many had gained respect on the street through their intervention in putting right what they deemed to be a wrong or by defending a more vulnerable person. Some even found themselves victims of rivals who wanted to rubbish the associated reputation and take over its mantle by taking them on and beating them up. Such actions invariably resulted in a vicious circle of violence as revenge attacks occurred involving more and more people, leading to virtual gang battles, a kind of precursor to today's football hooliganism where groups battle over a geographical area of power. Such groups consist of leaders, fighters, mischief makers and, on the fringes, the hangers on, the latter being the most devious and cunning of the group, capable of almost anything, apart from face to face physical combat. The options such individuals used ranged from deceit right through to the use of a varierty of weapons: blades, broken glass, machetes or firearms. Such is their insecurity that they generally need this armoury to defend themselves or to commit an unprovoked attack on an unsuspecting victim. There is no way that this sort can be regarded as hard men.

At the opposite end of the spectrum is the extortion merchant, a common bully who revels in the satisfaction of scaring people and putting the frighteners on them, forcing

The fiend of the Gorbals – Patrick Carraher.

them hand over money as a way of escaping the threatened violence or, more commonly, the complete destruction of their business. In London, the Kray twins were the perfect examples of an extortion gang, holding hundreds of well run businesses to ransom in the East End, and today their legacy continues with many people recalling how charming, good natured and friendly the pair were to their own kind, the East Ender.

In Glasgow the reputation of a psychopathic and alcoholic loner, Patrick Carraher, was fast becoming synonymous with extortion and severe violence, to such an extent that he became known as 'the Fiend of the Gorbals'.

Born into a good family in the Gorbals on 19 October 1906, Carraher had not the simplest of upbringings. At the age of four his mother died, leaving his father as the sole responsible adult in his life. Later, after his father remarried, the relationship between step- mother and step-son was strained from the outset. The woman showed little in the way of natural maternal instinct towards young Patrick, and as a result a divide was created between the pair. To make matters worse, his father, whom he once doted upon, supported his new wife and blamed Patrick for the woeful atmosphere in the home. His father took to severely beating and reprimanding him in order that he should snap out of dark moods. This had the opposite effect, causing Patrick to become isolated and introverted, effectively losing all trust and respect for his family.

It is said that by the age of fourteen Patrick Caraher had gained a decent reputation on the streets as a pugilist and a social deviant. Certainly, his home had become little more than a hotel – there was little in the way of sentimentality for the place where he would return infrequently, simply to catch up on sleep. By the age of seventeen he had become an established and hardened criminal, serving a fortnight in jail for assault. Thereafter followed several periods of detention, each relating to a variety of felonies committed over the years. Every new stint in prison made him more and more resilient to the ways of crime and, more pertinently, violent crime. Patrick learned the abilities and cunningness required of a street fighter and progressed into unadulterated violence, using a blade as his preferred method of choice. Carraher had become a very dangerous man indeed. Accompanying this dark side was an ever increasing penchant for alcohol. He was spiralling out of control at a rapid pace.

On 13 August 1938, after heavy days of drinking, he felt the need to see his ex-partner Kate Morgan who had ended their relationship due to his violent behaviour and attitude towards her. By chance he happened upon eighteen-year-old Margaret McNicol, a close friend of Kate. Carraher asked the girl to take a message to Kate, asking her to meet with him. Margaret knew it would be a pointless exercise as Kate Morgan had made it perfectly clear to all who knew her that she never wanted to see Patrick Carraher again and despised him. Diplomatically, Margaret McNicol explained to Carraher that it was no good as Kate wouldn't speak with him, so she refused to get involved, causing Carraher to burst into rage. Frightened, Margaret ran to the arms of her nineteen-year-old boyfriend, James Durie, who was a window cleaner by trade and was in the same street when McNicol first encountered Carraher. Immediately, a confrontation erupted with the drunken Carraher pulling at Margaret's arm, whilst her boyfriend tried to pull her free tugging at her other arm.

Margaret managed to break free of Carraher's hold and ran away from him, leaving her boyfriend alone to protect nothing but her dignity.

After the early sparring, Carraher moved onto more violent and unfair means of taking it out on the young boy now facing him. He pulled out a knife and lunged towards Jamie, who was wise enough to take to his heels along with Margaret and get away from the area and Patrick in particular.

The younger members of the Durie family were none too pleased with the manner in which Carraher had taken it upon himself to try to 'cut' Jamie and at once resolved to go in search if the man and to again confront him. Jamie quickly rounded up his twenty-four-year-old brother, John, Charles Morgan, the sixteen-year-old brother of his girlfriend and a family friend, Peter Howard, who was twenty-three. The group soon found their quarry and confronted him in Ballater Street, a short distance from Gorbals Cross. Jamie offered Carraher another chance; however, the drunken man refused, stating that through the amount he had drank he was currently in no fit state to offer a good challenge and told them to 'clear off'. An innocent passer-by, twenty-three-year-old James Sydney Shaw came across the scene, but drunk and full of mischief. Shaw joined in the abuse, and soon found himself on the wrong end of insults coming from Carraher. The ultimate humiliation suffered was when Carraher told Shaw to go away and to stop speaking 'like an Englishman'. Matters were about to deteriorate into physical violence when a policeman on patrol arrived in Ballater Street and told the men to leave it and to go and take a walk. Sensible advice, he too left the area. Without further ado, a scuffle ensued resulting in everyone focusing back on Shaw who was clutching his neck, blood spurting out from between his fingers. During the melee Peter Howard rushed to his aid and tried to help the wounded man. Carraher fled the scene.

James Shaw was haemorrhaging a lot of blood, pools dripping from his neck onto the pavement below. In a state of distress, Shaw tried to keep moving and, supported by Howard, kept going until he finally collapsed on the pavement outside a cinema. Another policeman on foot patrol found the two men and summoned an ambulance, also arresting Peter Howard on suspicion of the attack since when the officer arrived on the scene he saw that Howard was crouched over the prostrate victim and was covered in his blood. James Shaw was taken to the Royal Infirmary and died within minutes of being admitted.

The murder was cause for much gossip in the Gorbals district, especially how an innocent man had been arrested and further detained by the police despite the statement of a number of witnesses, who could positively state that he was innocent; and, further to this, named the guilty party. The gossip wasn't malicious, and it did of course get back to Patrick Carraher who felt threatened by the very nature of the atmosphere that was being aroused by public sympathy for the innocent Peter Howard. With this in mind, Carraher confessed to locals that he did use his blade to slash open the throat of James Shaw. He made sure that everyone knew he would hand himself into the police and clear an innocent man. Typical of his sort, he didn't, instead he threw the murder weapon into the River Clyde and went back to his room in Florence Street.

By now the pressure of public revolt was presenting itself to the police as they had the wrong man in custody and now looked more closely at the obvious facts and evidence available to them. The intelligence from the street pointed heavily towards Patrick Carraher's guilt. So he was duly arrested and charged with the murder and Peter Howard released. At his trial, his defence was that no one had seen him strike the killer blow and that he had been subject to abuse not only from Shaw but from the Durie family; also, he personally had not gone out looking for trouble. Subsequently, Carraher was found guilty of culpable homicide and sentenced to three years in Barlinnie Prison.

Carraher's release three years later was into a whole different world that was Glasgow, reeling from the pressures of war and an economy, focused on the hostilities, had seen a great many fit men being signed up to the war campaign. Furthermore, policing was greatly reduced and many of those that remained behind were more vulnerable and susceptible to criminal attack, be it housebreaking or street robbery. Within a few days, Carraher had met with a new love, Sarah Bonnar, and in doing so found himself a home. He also befriended Sarah's brother, Daniel, who was always up for earning a bit of easy money.

For weeks throughout 1943, the pair rampaged through the streets of Glasgow, robbing and attacking anyone who appeared an easy target. Where Carraher was concerned it was also a case of satiating his own appetite for violence, he had become a lost cause. On the night of 23 November 1943 Patrick Carraher committed his second murder, inflicting a four-inch gash in a man's throat. It all had happened, as usual, after a heavy bout of drinking, and became known after old confrontations occurred outside Cameron's Bar in Rottenrow – with the Gordon clan.

It was Daniel Bonnar who first bumped into the Gordons. Bonner had left Carraher and another man, Thomas Connolly Watt, in his flat with some 'female company' they had found and invited there. The Gordons meanwhile had amongst their ranks a number of deserters from the armed forces, men who couldn't handle the dangers, discipline and hard work a period of time in the hostilities forced upon servicemen.

Bonner had been made to flee the gang of the Gordons and ran to his sister's flat nearby. Angrily, he donned a woman's coat and grabbed an axe and returned to the street to sort out the Gordons once and for all. Word got to Patrick Carraher who was still in Bonnar's flat enjoying himself. All that ended when news that Daniel Bonnar was confronting the Gordon gang and he was armed with an axe. Swiftly, Carraher and Watt put on their coats and went out into the street in search of trouble. Carraher had with him a sharpened wood carver's chisel. The confrontation took place a few seconds later. Witnesses recalled seeing Carraher punch John Gordon in the face and head area. Unbeknown to anyone looking on, Carraher had in fact trained himself to hold a blade within his fist, concealing it from the opponent until it was too late and damage had been inflicted. John Gordon fell to the floor, blood pumping from a huge cut in his throat, and died a few minutes later at the Royal Infirmary. Carraher, as was his

Patrick Carraher.

method, slipped away into the night. He returned to Bonnar's flat in Rottenrow.

It didn't take too long for the rumours to begin to circulate and a taxi driver and a friend of Daniel Bonnar came to his flat to break the news that it was now murder, John Gordon having died at the infirmary. Patrick Carraher realised that he was done for if caught, so he handed over the murder weapon to the two men and told them to get rid of it by breaking it in two and dropping it into different drains in High Street where it would never be found. This was extremely trusting of him, as one of the men was a complete stranger.

The police soon had the evidence to make an arrest and had their man in custody within twenty-four hours. The evil reign of the Fiend of the Gorbals was over. So called friend Daniel Bonnar betrayed him to save his own neck, turning King's evidence, while Thomas Watt spoke of how Carraher had showed him the sharp-bladed chisel he had in his pocket en route to the crime, adding that Carraher had said: 'This will do for them'.

The evidence produced against him in court was overwhelming. Efforts were made to try to prove his insanity and having a persecution complex – convinced that people were hiding from, him in cupboards and behind doors – so he would frequently open them and check them. Whilst abnormal, it could hardly begin to determine why he was so violent and without moral substance.

The jury retired for twenty minutes before returning a verdict of guilty and the trial judge, Lord Russell, had no qualms about sentencing this clearly evil man to death. Subsequent appeals were dismissed and he was duly executed for the vicious crimes he committed upon many innocents in the city. Few were concerned about his fate, with the exception perhaps of his partner, Sarah Bonner.

CHAPTER 12

An Imperfect Murder: John Caldwell

1946

I t all began in a small first floor flat in Whitehall Street, Dennistoun, in March 1946. The flat was rented by a friendly lady called Mrs Pollock. Having been out of the flat for some time, she was extremely conscious where home security was concerned. She didn't like the look of some of the visitors who often called on other residents in the block where she lived. On this occasion not only had she secured her front door before leaving, but had also locked the inside doors. Her idea was to make it very difficult for an intruder to prowl from room to room without making a lot of noise, which would hopefully be sufficient to arouse the suspicion of a resident who could call the police. Imagine then, her shock when she returned home to find that the flat had been broken into, the intruder not your average burglar but was armed with a gun. The man had gained access by climbing a down pipe outside the house, smashing a small window and lifting the securing latch allowing them to lift the window. Once inside he was effectively trapped by the locked inner doors secured by Mrs Pollock. Whoever it was, on finding one of the doors locked had fired a round into one the locks in a desperate attempt to open it and get out. Mrs Pollock called the police who duly attended and took details, informing the shocked victim that it was more than likely going to be a job for the Criminal Investigation Department (CID) to deal with, since the use of a firearm was deemed a more serious offence not usually investigated by uniformed officers. A formal search of the flat was carried out and fingerprint dust coated on surfaces where the intruder may have left a print. No alien fingerprints were recovered from the flat.

Precisely a week later another Dennistoun flat was broken into, this time in Golfhill Drive. Mrs Morgan returned home to find a man going through some of her property, and empty jewellery boxes were strewn around the bedroom. She confronted the man who was ransacking her possessions. He seemed to care little that she was there and produced a revolver from his pocket, threatening to shoot her. She decided to back away and asked him to leave, which he did. The police arrived and once again the flat was dusted for fingerprints. This time they were fortunate, on a piece of glass was a partial print. Mrs Morgan provided a description of the intruder, a man aged between twenty to twenty-five years, around five feet six inches tall, slim-built, pale-faced and wearing a grey overcoat, white scarf and a cap. Mrs Morgan also said that she felt that it was hardly the sort of man one would expect to be acting in such a manner.

The following day another incident of housebreaking took place, this time at the home of Mr and Mrs Deekan of 524 Edinburgh Road, in the city. The couple had gone out to the cinema for the evening. By 8.25 pm they were on their way home and were crossing the road in front of their house when Mr Deekan noticed a light on in their upstairs room, a light that he was certain wasn't on when the couple left home that evening. He instructed his wife to go next door and fetch an ex-Glasgow police Detective Sergeant, James Straiton. Mrs Straiton told the ex-cop that her husband believed they had intruders in the house and to come at once. Straiton dressed more appropriately and grabbed his old police truncheon before making his way to number 524.

Meanwhile, Mr Deekan, keen not to disturb and frighten off the invader, had made his way to the rear of the house and quietly climbed in through a ground floor window, to the darkened hallway that led to the front door which gave access to the upper floors via the staircase. He felt insecure in the darkness, hearing the clumping noises of the intruder searching for valuables. Finally, he could take no more and he switched on the staircase and hall light. Looking up the stairs,

Deekan saw two men at the top. He turned to the front door, opened it and stepped outside, awaiting the arrival of James Straiton. Within seconds both intruders had leapt down the stairs and were making their way out of the house via the front door. The first man down the stairs appeared in the hallway armed with a revolver in each hand. James Straiton arrived just in time to see the first intruder fire off a shot from one of the guns, aimed at Deekan but it missed its target.

Both Deekan and Straiton confronted the intruders and began to tussle with them, Straiton launching in with his truncheon, striking the gunman over the head and momentarily stunning him. The fight was one of life and death and a further round was fired off during the fracas, hitting Straiton in the midriff, instantly causing him to buckle and fall to the floor. He was fatally injured. Deekan was shocked by the incident and stopped fighting in order to help his neighbour. The two intruders made their escape into the night, discarding one of the two revolvers as they did so. It was later ascertained that this weapon actually belonged to Deekan and was part of the stolen booty removed by the gunman during the raid on his house.

The police were on scene within minutes, the gunman and his accomplice had, for now, escaped. James Straiton was in a bad way, blood and trauma from the severity of the gunshot wound had caused him to go into shock. His breathing was erratic and it was clear that he was not going to survive this attack. He passed away shortly after.

A full-scale murder investigation was now under way. A thorough search of the property and surrounding area revealed a number of clues, including a pair of shoes which had been left at the foot of a downpipe in the garden of the Deekan home. This of course meant that one of the intruders had made his getaway in his stocking feet, prompting the police to ask for anyone seeing a fleeing man in his stocking feet on the night in question to come forward. Several reports were received but none sufficiently positive to glean any further evidence.

Entry had been gained into the property by the intruders climbing the downpipe and breaking a first floor window before getting into the house. Three spent cartridges, each fired from a .45 revolver, were also recovered from the grounds, and it was proven that these were not fired from the gun belonging to Deekan. The intruders left no fingerprints in the house and were clearly wearing loves during the raid. In describing the man that shot and killed Straiton, Deekan said that he was between five foot three inches and five foot six inches tall, had a thin face, long nose and was wearing a greyish tweed-type coat; he also wore a white scarf. Neither intruder wore a hat or cap. There were no other distinguishing features to help reveal the mans identity.

For a whole week, Detective Chief Superintendent Bill Ewing laboured to moving the investigation forward. Every avenue was been explored, but without fingerprints or other tell-tale evidence then the case was stuck. He sought the advice of Detective Superintendent McIllwrick who asked Ewing to recount the situation to him. Once this had been done, McIllwrick advised Ewing to use the new card index system he had created, where the *modus operandi* of all known offenders in Glasgow had been meticulously recorded, along with fingerprints and other useful intelligence.

McIllwrick recalled how there had been three housebreaking incidents in the Dennistoun area in recent weeks. Each time, the intruders had climbed a drain pipe to the first floor where they gained access, a revolver had been used and, on two occasions, the intruder was seen to be wearing a white scarf. He advised Ewing to get his officers to search to see if any previous incidents with any similar trademarks had occurred. With the partial fingerprint that had been collected from Golfhill Drive crime scene, he should get his officers to go through the same system in search of an identical print that may be on file.

The search was to prove useful, from the modus operandi files came the names of some 450 known criminals who had used any one of the methods of entry in order to houses. To hone it down further, 450 fingerprint files matching the criminals highlighted were withdrawn for physical analysis. It was clearly going to be a painstaking and laborious task but one that might well provide no positive identification of the offenders.

Glasgow High Court.

It was Detective Constable Douglas Hamilton who first let out a cry of excitement, a thumbprint he was holding provided a perfect match to the partial print found at Golfhill Drive. Other officers checked the two prints, then checked them again. There was no doubt about it, the print belonged to the same person. Within half an hour of the fingerprint card index system being used, Bill Ewing was receiving the telephone call he had been waiting for. The thumbprint was confirmed as being that of twenty-year-old John Caldwell of Fielden Street, Bridgeton. Ewing thanked the officers and told them to stand down and report for duty the next day.

The following morning, John Caldwell's criminal antecedents were checked out. He was known to be violent, the police also knew that he was armed and therefore dangerous. A team was put together and briefed. Caldwell had to be brought to justice, Ewing did not want the killer of an ex-colleague and such a brutal criminal to get away. Minutes later, John Caldwell was overpowered and arrested by a team of detectives at his home address, for the murder of James Straiton. He had no chance to use the firearm to defend himself and was quickly clamped in handcuffs and taken to the police station for interview. It was soon revealed that the bullet extracted from the door lock in the flat in Whitehall Street had been fired by the same weapon that had shot and killed James Straiton. Furthermore, the shoes found at the scene of the Edinburgh Road killing were confirmed as belonging to Caldwell. It was a strong and positive stream of evidence that would prove the case in court.

Caldwell informed the police that his accomplice was a fifteen-year-old youth who was described as mentally defective. With this in mind the prosecution preferred no charges against him, as he was easily led and controlled by Caldwell.

The case against Caldwell was heard at the High Court in Glasgow on 26 June 1946, when he was tried on charges of murder and attempted murder. The jury had no reservations about the validity of each offence and found him guilty on both accounts. In desperation he appealed against the judgment of the death penalty, but it was dismissed. Caldwell was hanged on the morning of 10 August 1946.

CHAPTER 13

The Killer Cop:
James Ronald Robertson

1950

Glasgow police, like other United Kingdom police forces, has had during its formative years, its fair share of individual officers who display little in the way of integrity and have shown themselves to be utterly criminal in their actions. The killer in this case is a man who held a responsible position, not only professionally but as a husband and father too. He continually lied to those closest to him, those same people who cared so much for him, and were deceived.

Glasgow in 1950 was a hardworking and developing city, the memories of the war fast receding as Scotland as a whole was in a state of total regeneration both economically and physically. Law and order was essential to community development and integration and the service of the police was the backbone to such activity. Imagine then, the public and professional outrage when a serving police officer was proven in a court of law to be a liar and a killer.

Police constable 138D James Ronald Robertson, at just thirty-three years of age, standing at six foot one inch, and of a strong muscular build, was originally viewed by his peers as a good and positive officer. Teetotal and a non-smoker, he was seen as a man who did things properly, was respectful of his family roots and commitments dating back to his upbringing; and was raised in a religious household. To all intents and purposes he had a very good life. Robertson had, by 1950, received two commendations from the Chief Constable for his endeavours in bringing offenders to justice.

PC Robertson – killer.

In the early hours of the morning of 28 July 1950, PC Robertson, on night duty, was requested to make the call to his control room, reporting his beat area as correct and to complete the log book, evidencing the fact that he was patrolling his beat. He was instructed to insert into the logbook at the Cumberland Street signal box the following entry:

> *At 1250 am today a woman was knocked down and fatally injured in Prospecthill Road near Aikenhead Road. The motor car, believed to be a small blue Austin, maybe 10hp, was driven by a man wearing a light fawn Burberry coat. The car did not stop and was last seen driving city-wards in Aikenhead Road.*

Clearly, it was a particularly nasty incident and the police were desperate to catch the gutless offender.

Earlier that morning, a taxi driver driving along Prospecthill Road in his cab, had been the first person to come across the tragic scene. The headlights of his vehicle picked up the motionless body that lay in the road, about three feet from the kerb. Stopping and getting out to check to see if it was a drunk, the driver soon realised that he was looking a horrendously disfigured young woman. One look at her injuries left him in little doubt that she was dead. Within seconds a Corporation lorry pulled up. The driver told the taxi driver that he and his work colleagues had past the scene about ten minutes earlier when a black saloon car had been parked up on the very spot. It was parked without any lights on and was notable because it was so far away from the kerb and had caused him as the driver to swerve round it. One of the passengers in the lorry had commented as they passed the parked saloon that he thought he had seen a body lying in the road behind the car. The lorry driver dismissed the comment and continued on his way.

The police were soon on the scene, a car with Constable William Keven, a vastly experienced and respected officer who had investigated countless road traffic accidents, took control of the accident site. He noted the condition of the road and, importantly, the victim. The woman had auburn hair, matted with blood, and wore a light coloured coat over a red dress. She lay on her back, her legs crossed above the knee and with her arms laid by her side. Her shoes were laying some distance away from the body. Dentures, broken and smashed, lay in pieces, clearly forced from her mouth by the collision of her head with the car and the road. The woman's outer clothing was saturated in blood and oil.

Of the scene itself the constable was mystified by the fact that there was no evidence of a road traffic accident: no smashed headlight glass, no dropped hardened mud that gathers within inner wheel arches and drops off with impact, no vehicle debris of any sort could be found. Two curious skid/brake marks had been left on the road surface. One was in a straight line, the other curved and both met. The body of the dead woman lay across these marks. Further examination of these revealed a good deal more about the incident.

It was evident that a vehicle travelling westerly along Prospecthill Road had left one of the brake marks, streaked at their beginning then more complete as they continued to the vehicle's stopping place. The curved marks however, had been made by a vehicle travelling in the opposite direction. Further to this, PC Keven believed that the body had been trapped beneath the vehicle and dragged along its underside, the driver having seemingly stopped and reversed, causing more damage to the trapped body. He believed it to be murder – the first time a car had been assigned as a murder weapon in Glasgow's criminal history.

By the time the press had got hold of the story and printed details of a 'hit and run' and requested that anyone who knew a woman who had not returned home since the previous evening to get in touch with the police, matters had moved on. The murder squad became involved and soon a young woman came forward to positively identify the dead female, whom she had been babysitting for the previous night. The victim was Catherine McCluskey, a forty-year-old single mother of two children. Police were keen to piece together the woman's movements on the night of her death and beforehand. A number of the dead woman's friends were interviewed by detectives and soon a picture began to emerge that did not auger too well for the Glasgow police force. A number of female friends of Catherine revealed that she was in a relationship with a married police officer that they simply knew as 'Robertson'. He had by all accounts promised Catherine that his marriage was over and that he was about to leave the family home. He wanted to find somewhere for both he and Catherine to move into as the family he really wanted. Other witnesses spoke of seeing Catherine being driven around in a black car by a uniformed policeman.

The police investigation was internalised as any officer bearing the surname Robertson was sought out. It didn't take too long for the name James Robertson to emerge. The police officer had in more recent times seemingly lost the plot, under investigation for being absent from his beat in the Gorbals area on two occasions.

Robertson was arrested on suspicion of murder. He claimed he was innocent and used as his alibi the fact that he was on duty as a policeman on the night of the murder, therefore could not have killed the woman. It soon came to light that, as before, he had gone missing from his beat area that evening.

He continued to deny murder, however the evidence that continued to emerge was more than sufficiently damning.

Within hours the police had set up an identity parade, the first of its kind in the history of crime around the globe for it featured a complete line up of fully uniformed police officers. A check of the car used by Robertson revealed that it was running on false number plates and was in fact reported stolen earlier on the evening of the crime. Constable James Robertson was arrested and charged with the theft of the car, a charge that was quickly followed by murder. Friends of the dead woman were called to try to identify the officer they had seen with Catherine. Robertson was picked out of the resultant identity parades. Without further ado he was transported to Barlinnie prison where he was held awaiting trial for murder.

By the time of his trial, on 6 November 1950, Robertson had lost all public sympathy, but the press had done all that the police had asked in not pre-empting his guilt beforehand. However, friends of the two victims in this sad situation, Catherine McCluskey and James Robertson's wife, were outspoken in their condemnation of the police officer.

The trial itself was held in the North Court of the Glasgow High Court and was meticulously handled by Lord Keith who had before him some of the most revered legal experts in Scotland, with leading barristers representing both the prosecution and the defence. For the Crown there was the Advocate Depute, Mr Harold Lees KC assisted by Advocate Ian Robertson. For the defence there was John Cameron KC and Michael Kissen.

The undeniable and sickening evidence against James Robertson came out. It was alleged that he had met with Catherine McCluskey on the night in question and had tried to end their relationship, a matter that greatly upset her and caused her much emotional turmoil, especially as Robertson was the father of her second child. Whether she made threats to reveal all or not was never confirmed. However, it seemed likely that she would not simply accept the termination of the relationship so easily. Certainly something had caused Robertson to snap.

It was alleged that he first struck Catherine McCluskey over the head with his truncheon or rendered her unconscious by other means. He then ran her over and reversed the stolen car back over her again to ensure her death, faking the murder scene to replicate a hit and run accident. One by one the witnesses came forward. Friends of the murdered woman told of how she would talk of her policeman boyfriend and how he was father of her second child. As if that was not sufficient, an official representing the National Assistance Board from whom she was claiming allowances told the court how she had refused to identify and name the father of her second child, though had revealed that it was a married police officer.

A car showroom salesman provided evidence that the motor vehicle in which the crime was committed was stolen from his premises, engine and radio serial numbers proving the case. One of Robertson's work colleagues, a fellow officer on the same number 8 beat area, stated that Robertson had taken him out onto the beat area in the car he now knew to be stolen, which he had parked in a lane nearby. He had left his colleague at around 11.00 pm that evening, saying that he had to 'take a blonde home'. Later, Robertson had failed to turn up at a serious incident, eventually arriving back on his beat at twenty minutes past midnight. He had been absent for one hour twenty minutes. Forensic evidence proved that Robertson had been in the stolen car and had been driving it.

Eventually, on the second day of the trial, Robertson was called to answer the allegations made against him. He spoke of his antecedents, being a police officer for five years and having first met Catherine McCluskey in 1949. He denied stealing the car, claiming that he had seen it abandoned on waste ground for a number of days then eventually decided to take it for a run. He later made up false number plates, and used the vehicle on a regular basis. He further claimed that he had met Catherine on the night in question and driven her round for a time. She had asked to be dropped off in Neilston, where he told her he could not do it as he was supposed to be at work. She had got upset and cried, so he pacified her before dropping her off in Prospecthill Road. He had then driven off but had not noticed knocking her over. He did not like to leave her alone and reversed back to where he dropped her off and noticed a sudden change in the exhaust noise. He had stopped the car and got out to see what the noise was, he then saw the face of Catherine McCluskey looking up at him from beneath the car running board, her mouth filled with blood. Panic stricken, he drove off. After two hours and nineteen minutes, Robertson returned to dock.

The trial continued and, several days later, the jury retired to assess the evidence. It took them just one hour of deliberating before they returned to the courtroom and provided a unanimous guilty verdict. Robertson stood confidently in the dock as sentencing was passed upon him, death by execution. Immediately, the Robertson defence team lodged a formal appeal but it was dismissed. Despite this, Robertson bragged to fellow inmates in prison that he would not hang.

On 16 December 1950, James Robertson was hanged at Barlinnie Prison, a convicted liar, thief and a killer. It is said that he was severely affected by grief on the night prior to his execution. His suffering could never have been as great as that of his victim. One can only hope that the indifference he displayed in the commission of his crime was shown to him on his journey to the gallows.

CHAPTER 14

Who Killed Betty?

1952

At about 7.00 pm, in the evening of 7 October 1952, Mrs Alexander of 43 Buccleugh Street, Glasgow went out to call for her four-and-a-half-year-old daughter who, like so many other children, was used to playing out in the street. It was bath time, then bed for the fresh-faced innocent young child with fair curly hair and beautiful blue eyes. Betty was a good girl and was always close to the house so when Mrs Alexander's cursory glance into the street went unheeded, she believed that Betty had wandered back into the terraced family home. A search of the house yielded nothing, so the mother, now just beginning to feel the anxiety levels rising in her body, stepped out into the street and made a more concerted effort to find her daughter. She called on neighbours in case the child had gone into one of their homes with a playing friend. No one it seemed had seen Betty or knew of her whereabouts.

Within an hour, a search party had been formed consisting of friends and neighbours as surrounding streets and alleys were patrolled and checked, door upon door was knocked upon as the searchers asked anyone and everyone if they had seen the missing little girl. The police from the Northern Division had been notified from the outset and helped coordinate the search task. Checks were made with local hospitals in case Betty had been taken there. There was no trace of the little girl anywhere. For two days and nights police officers scoured the district, spoke with taxi drivers, bus drivers and stopped travellers passing through the area, all without success. Eventually, on 9 October, the search and investigation stepped up when the Criminal Investigation Department got involved and took control of the case. The introduction of the CID meant that the investigating authorities were now considering more sinister notions as to Betty Alexander's disappearance.

The local press had already alerted of the circumstances surrounding the missing child and did all they could to help broadcast descriptions and details. Finally, every police officer in the city of Glasgow was called in for the most comprehensive missing person search carried out up to that time. Dustbins were checked, car drivers asked to open their boots, and sheds and outhouses were checked at every house in the city. Photographs of Betty were strategically placed throughout Glasgow in the hope that the image might jog someone's memory of seeing the little girl. Every police officer studied the picture and maintained the child's soft features at the front of their mind. Everyday policing for criminal activities took second place to finding little Betty.

Even the criminal classes themselves got involved in the search and pooled information and knowledge to finger any known 'ponces' that they knew lived in the city or nearby who may have abducted the child for their own devices. Paedophiles and child sex offenders since time immemorial have been classed as the lowest of low throughout society, pariahs and deviants they are regarded as being 'sick' and outcasts of a normal society. The criminal underworld has a strict code of conduct, whereby sex crimes and specifically those committed against children are abhorred, any person so convicted and sentenced to imprisonment physically attacked and beaten at the first opportunity by fellow inmates. Hence today such criminal types often receive official protection whilst in custody or incarcerated or are placed in solitary units, well away from the prison population.

On 10 October 1952, the search for Betty Alexander was brought to a sudden and abrupt end. Agnes Hunter, a cleaner in the hospital dispensary close to the Alexander home, took some carpets out into the rear yard. She intended to hang these over the washing line and beat the dust from them. As she hung the carpets out she noticed a bundle lying close to the back steps. Agnes disliked mess and, believing that someone had dumped an old bundle of rags and clothes and other detritus there, went over to take a look with the intention of cleaning it up. As she approached the bundle she jumped back in horror and screamed out. It was the body of little Betty Alexander.

The police were quickly on the scene. It was clear that the child had been dead for some time, there was clear evidence of 'assault' and that Betty had died of suffocation. Detective Chief Superintendent Gilbert McIllwrick was senior officer on the case. A hardened cop, McIllwrick had seen it all and there was few things his professional role could uncover that would surprise or shock him. But seeing the tiny body of Betty Alexander hurt him, stunned by the ferocity and nature of the crime and he vowed to do all he could to bring the perpetrator (or perpetrators) to justice. He sealed off the rear yard and all access and egress points nearby. He put local people under voluntary house arrest, as he didn't want anyone leaving the area before they were interviewed and cleared of suspicion. Everyone had to be a suspect.

McIllwrick then pulled together a team of his best detectives, instructing them to use every resource available to question local people; others were told to identify, locate and question known sex offenders or anyone with suspicious antecedents that lived in the area. It seemed clear to McIllwrick that the killer or killers were local. The placement of the body so close to the scene of its disappearance tended to support the fact that Betty had been killed inside someone's home, abused then dumped in the yard during the darkness of night when there was no one around. A police tracker dog was brought to the yard. However, with so many different scents now suffocating the original source the animal made very little in the way of progress. The Identification Bureau, a predecessor of the modern day forensics team scoured the scene for clues; everything that could yield potential was dusted for fingerprints, resulting in the removal of a wooden door and a step. The yard door actually yielded a partial fingerprint. Great efforts were made to try to trace it through the official fingerprint records held by the police, but sadly this was not possible. Despite this, the police were desperate to find the killer(s). By the very nature of the assault they knew a man had to be involved, therefore they asked all local men who lived in the neighbourhood to voluntarily provide fingerprints in order to release them from further enquiries. A thousand adult males agreed to the police request, not one provided a direct match to the partial print. Finally, the police concluded that the print could have been alien and innocent to the investigation.

Each day new information was received by the police who had asked that anything, no matter how minor or menial it may appear to be, should be conveyed to the investigating police officers. Several reports from independent sources indicated that, earlier that evening, Betty had been seen in the company of a man, described as being short and dark. The description got no better and sadly the reports could not be progressed any further. Other reports claimed that Betty had been seen in a car with man; however, this was eventually dismissed as a killer with a car had the means to deposit the remains well away from the scene of the abduction. The police still believed that the killer lived locally and possibly knew Betty Alexander.

One piece of intelligence that determined more positive investigations was that Betty had been seen stroking and playing with a white-haired dog. White animal hairs, presumably from a dog, had actually been found on her clothing, a fact that the police were holding back as it was viewed as a potential clue. When the hairs were examined more closely it was discovered that each had a black tip to it. Now it was the turn of police officers to root out every dog in the district and to take sample hair from it. Not an easy task as there was many stray animals to check.

A breakthrough was achieved when an officer found the dog in question, traced to a nearby house in Buccleugh Lane; but a search of the property revealed no evidence to indicate that Betty had been to the house or that the animal's owner was in any way involved with the crime. He provided suitable alibis and stated that his dog was well known in the area and children generally patted and cuddled it when they saw it. As a result of this, several children were spoken to and confirmed their knowledge of the popular white dog. Once again, the police were left with nothing to go on, albeit one suspects that the matter relating to the dog hairs discovered on the remains and in the fabric of the child's clothing perhaps deserved greater examination and investigation than time and pressure permitted.

A telephone call received by the police on 15 October was curious to say the least. It was from a man who confessed to the murder and provided detail of the crime. It is a well known fact that when such high profile crimes do occur then all kinds of people find themselves attracted to them, individuals who have no knowledge or involvement often confess to committing the crime, almost as if they yearn for the attention. Thankfully, experienced police officers can spot the attention seekers at an early stage; hence little time is wasted on their needs. However, in this instance, the police were sufficiently intrigued as to have the man arrested and further questioned. Unfortunately, within a short space of time it became clear that he was not the killer since all the information and quotes he had made had been lifted from newspaper reports. When probed further, he couldn't provide anything, nor did he accurately describe the scene where Betty's remains were deposited, so he was nothing but a liar. The man was released and warned about his future conduct.

Two men form the same family (father and son) were branded by locals as murder suspects, as they were known to trawl the streets at curious hours and act in a furtive and curious manner. One local woman described them as having an 'odd' look about them. The rumour mill soon began to grind out tales surrounding the activities of the men resulting in the pair of them suffering great verbal and physical abuse whenever they were abroad in the area. One of the two men was actually hit with a brick that had been thrown at him by a group of adults. He reported the matter and the abusive rumours to the police, but they could do little to prevent the acidic tales from circulating. Finally, in October 1952, the family, consisting of father, mother and son were invited to visit the police station and offer themselves up for questioning and examination. This news quickly filtered back to the Buccleugh Street community and, as is generally the case, changed in its content and accuracy. It was widely anticipated the family would be charged with the murder and associated crimes.

Detective Superintendent McIllwrick and the Procurator Fiscal questioned the family throughout the night and into the following morning. When the news broke that none of the family had been arrested or charged with any crime, it left a sense of unease throughout the district. The majority believed them to be guilty of the crime and were shocked that they were released, others sensed that mass hysteria was driving people to condemn anyone who they felt didn't fit in with their perception of how life should be, as the killer. After three weeks of solid police enquiries and, after providing every available police resource to the investigation, the authorities were no further forward. Policing had to return to normality, thus the investigation was gradually wound down and seemingly disappearing with it was the last remaining chance that the killer (or killers) of Betty Alexander would be brought to justice. To this very day it still remains a mystery.

CHAPTER 15

Serial Killer Who Fed the Cat: Peter Manuel

1956/57

There are those who say that he was insane, others believe him to have been just plain evil, while many think him to have simply been a selfish and scheming man who would stop at nothing to get what he wanted. Quite what that was – well, not even he could provide a sensible answer. Peter Thomas Anthony Manuel was born at the Misere Cordia Hospital, in Manhatton, New York on 15 March 1927, one of three children to Samuel Manuel and his wife Bridget. Peter was the middle child. With British roots, the

Murder house, home of the Watt family.

The serial killer, Peter Manuel.

family had always intended to return back to these shores and, a few years later, they moved back home, to Coventry, then to Birkenshaw, near Uddingston, in Lanarkshire.

The young Peter Manuel was not one to make friends easily. Despite his tender years he was forming a bad reputation as being something of a troublemaker within his peer group. By the age of ten Peter had brought embarrassment upon his family when he was reported for petty theft from the local shops. It may only have been cigarettess and confectionary, however the basic principals of theft are precisely the same. The fact that he was smoking at such a young age suggests the child was already in need of help, gradually moving out of control. Within a year he found himself on probation as matters deteriorated, having broken into a shop, again for cigarettes. The leniency of any real punishment and therefore a potential deterrent did nothing to help rehabilitate this young boy. For him, a life of crime offered a good deal more in the way of material reward and, as he matured in age (but not in common sense) he became far more shrewd and astute about the way he carried out his criminal acitvity. Between the age of eleven and eighteen young Manuel spent much of his time in approved schools and Borstal whch hardened to a life of crime. He lived life on the edge, enjoying the thrill of housebreaking, whether the victim was present or not. He carried out such crimes primarily at night. However, as he became more greedy, he realised that propertes stood empty for much of the day whilst the owners were out at work. It wasn't as if he was an expert at such crimes, as he often found himself caught in the act; but with no real punishment meted out he would return to crime, often within hours of being released from police custody.

At the age of fifteen he carried out an awful attack on a young girl at Ainsdale in Southport. The girl had returned home from a nightshift at the local munitions factory. Drawing the blackout curtains in her room, she went to her bed. A few hours later, the girl was awakened by a seering pain rushing through her head. Looking up from her pillow she saw a boy stood over her, in his hand a hammer with a handkerchief wrapped around its handle (to protect him from leaving fingerprints). He rained down several blows to the girl's head before making off with her purse and its paltry contents. It was aneedless attack since the sleeping girl offered no threat to the housebreaking Manuel. The police and the troops were given an excellent description of the young man and various witnesses saw him flee the scene. He was found shortly after, hiding in some woods. The result was a charge of assault and two individual accounts of burglary. He was sent to yet another Approved School, this time in Yorkshire.

During his spell at the Approved School he took to secreting himself away in obscure hiding places. On one occasion he hid in a timy space behind a Christmas crib within the school. He was reported missing and caused a nationwide police search. He did finally abscond and was caught in Glasgow. The Approved School was not the right place for the wild Peter Manuel and he made two further escapes. On the second he again broke into a house and armed himself with a dagger, before again being caught. This time he received a term of imprisonment in Leeds' Armley prison.

Upon his release there followed more crime and associated issues wherever he went. Attracted by the crowds and excitement of Blackpool during he summer, he stopped at the town for several months, getting involved with local hoodlums and gangs, turning over the easy picking that were tourists. His negative attitude got him into trouble many times with local gangs and it is claimed that he received several beatings for his untoward activities in their area. Eventually, he became well known to the local police and was often spoken to regarding crimes. One such occasion saw him identified by a local gang for the burglary of an office. He was arrested and charged but at court was found not guilty. As he left he received the 'friendly' warning from some of the local criminal fraternity that his time in the town was over and he should move on for his own safety.

Manuel returned to his family home in Scotland and immediately set about more criminal activity. Had psychological profilers been available to the Glasgow police at this time then Peter Manuel would not doubt have been flagged up as a real danger to society.

Some of the incidents and crimes that had occurred during his time in the approved schools had sexual undertones, victims of his attacks had their underwear pulled down, exposing and displaying sexual parts, all part of his feeling of power. There was another incident involving a female teacher who was threatends by Manuel with a knife which he held to her throat. He pulled down the womans underwear and looked at her, yet not once up to that time did he physically interfere with his victims. Had such a modus operandi been commuincated across police forces and other authorities then the activities of Peter Manuel may well have come to light sooner.

His early time in Scotland was spent as a predator, with reports that he would wander quiet country lanes and practice using his blade on sheep and cattle. This from a man who displayed a softer side to his personality when around the family pet alsation, Rusty. All the time he continued his housebreaking routines, stealing money and any valuables he could sell on to his fellow criminals. At one stage he appeared in court on fifteen separate housebreaking charges and was incredibly released on bail. During this time his anger towards society, and in particular women, reached new heights. While on bail, he viciously attacked a pregnant woman. Beating her unconscious and dragging her down onto a railway embankment, there he indecently assaulted and raped her. Manuel was caught through some clever detective work, his description recognized but when police questioned him, he denied the attack. However, soil found in the turn-up of his trousers matched that at the scene of the crime, so he was charged with rape and duly sentenced to twelve months' imprisonment on the fifteen housebreaking charges and eight years for the rape, to be served at Peterhead Prison.

Inside prison, as a pathological liar, he created for himself a life of deceit and crime in an attempt to impress some of the more hardened lags, even creating a successful boxing career for himself. To further influence this image he attacked two prison officers, receiving spells in solitary confinement for doing so. Despite all his efforts, he was regarded by those who knew him inside as a petty criminal with a big ego and of no substance. As such, suffering nothing but derision from his fellow prison inmates, this seriously affected him psychologically. Inside his head he was a seething mass of anger, desperate to prove to society, be it generally or from the criminal fraternity, that he was important and powerful, not scared of the establishment.

On Manuel's release he made efforts to prove to his devoutly Catholic family that he was on the road to complete rehabilitation, taking up temporary work on the railways and was employed by the council as a dustman and a labourer. In July 1955 all that went out of the window as he brutally attacked a young girl returning home from a dance. Arrested and charged, his family made efforts to prove insanity, that he was unfit to plead. He conducted his own defence at the subsequent trial where the victim revealed that he had led her through fields and raped her, afterwards saying: 'He told me he had been watching television that night when he had a sudden impulse to cut soemone's head off and bury them.' Incredibly, the jury found the charge against him not proven and he walked free from the court.

By now his family had seen enough to know that Peter needed help, his behaviour, although good at home was erratic when he was out. The death of the family pet dog, Rusty, killed in a road accident sent him into a crazed rage as he threatened to hunt down the offending driver and kill him. Despite the family's pleas to the authorities to have their son examined by a psychiatrist, nothing happened. Albeit, the police were keeping a more than watchful eye on him.

Peter Manuel's desire to be important continued. He was slighlty more discreet in his latest venture, but nonetheless a need to be respected by the police and law enforcement agencies was evident. He started to write and send letters to the police claiming to have indepth knowledge about local crimes. The fact that many of the details contained within these missives were grossly inaccurate mattered little, the police were onto him, but still they were not close enough.

On 2 January 1956, seventeen-year-old Anne Kneilands disappeared after leaving her East Kilbride home enroute to a dance. She was regarded as a pleasant and pretty young girl with a good family upbringing and no known vices. Her failure to return home was completely out of character for her, alerting her parents and the police that something sinister may have happened. Two days later she was found dead, her battered remains close to the fifth tee of East Kilbride golf course. Examination of the scene revealed that she had probably been chased through a nearby wood then attacked and killed. The police trail ended there, but the underworld soon put it out the details of the man responsible.

Peter Manuel had been working near the scene of the murder, and the day after crime he had scratches on his face. The police moved in, searching his home and checking his clothing. By now, Manuel had developed a criminal cunning that on this occasion outwitted the police, as there was no evidence found to link or associate him with the crime, and he claimed the scratches on his face were caused through a brawl in a bar.

On 17 September 1956 police were called to a bungalow in Fennsbank Avenue, High Burnside, Rutherglen. Inside the house, officers found the bodies of Marion Watt, her sixteen-year-old daughter Vivienne Watt and Mrs Margaret Brown (sister of Marion Watt). Each of the victims had been shot through the head. The house was a mess, with obvious signs of a struggle, particularly in Vivienne's room. Vivienne's pants had been removed leaving her exposed. After the attack it seemed clear that the killer had been calm enough to eat some food before leaving the scene.

Once again, word on the street was that Peter Manuel was the killer. The police swooped and carried out an intense search of the family home, claiming that they believed Manuel to have a firearm in his possession, but no such weapon was found. The local community was in uproar, the Watt family had been executed within the sanctuary of their own home, they had no known enemies, albeit William Watt was an ex-policeman, yet William Watt wasn't at home when the attack occurred. Suddenly the focus of the police investigation turned to William Watt, a loving husband and father with no record of violence nor reason to kill his own family.

At the time of the killings, William Watt had in fact been away in a different part of Scotland, Lochgilphead, Argyll, on a fishing break. The police arrested him, claiming that he had driven home through the night, executed his family and returned back to the hotel and his fishing. The poor man was clearly suffering with the murder of his entire family and few believed him to have been the assassin, everyone it seems except the police, though to be fair, a worker on the Renfrew Ferry came forward and stated that he recognised Watt who had travelled on the ferry on the night of murder .

Watt was detained in Barlinnie prison pending furtherpolice investigations. Meanwhile, Peter Manuel was also incarcerated in Barlinnie prison, committed to an eighteen month sentence for breaking into a canteen. Once again, Manuel's desire for attention came to the fore, as he began to send letters to William Watt's lawyer, Lawrence Dowdall. In these, Manuel detailed how Watt was innocent because another prisoner had confessed to him that he had killed the Watt family. The letters contained detailed descriptions of the inside of the Watt home, details that could only be known to someone who had been in the premises. In addition to this he related sensitive material concerning the crime. One fact that had not previously been publicly released was that one of the victims had been shot in the head twice.

Manuel revealed this information. The lawyer moved swiftly and used the 'new' facts to accomplish the release of William Watt from custody. Peter Manuel was quizzed about the information contained within the letters, police searched his home and his room but once again there was nothing in the way of direct evidence to link him with the murders.

Manuel was released from prison in November 1957 and at once contacted newspapers in an attempt to sell the new facts of the case to them. Few were interested in his patter. He was treated as non-important and again realised that he had no power to influence on society. Just over a week later, for no reason, he shot a taxi driver, Sidney Dunn, in the back of the head, before slitting his throat wide open. This occurred close to the village of Edmundbyers in Durham. The only clue the police had was that when he had priced up a fare from outside Newcastle railways station, the man had talked with a strong Scottish accent.

Twenty days later, on 28 December 1957, a seventeen-year-old schoolgirl, Isabelle Cooke, left her Carrick Drive home to catch a bus to a school dance. She took a short cut through some fields near her Mount Vernon home. It was also close to

Isabelle Cooke, murder victim.

the home of Peter Manuel. Isabelle was never again seen alive. A search was carried using all the emergency services and the public, resulting in a shoe and her handbag was recovered, while frogmen found items of her clothing from the River Calder, about one mile from the scene of the crime. The investigating authorities were at aloss as to where the body could be and even considered that it may have been thrown from a bridge into a goods train travelling south into England. This theory was further supported when a railway worker came forward and gave a description of a man he saw loitering close to a branch line on the night Isabelle disappeared, described as 'aged about thirty-five, five foot six inches tall, dark hair and wearing a dark coat'. Whilst all this activity was taking place, three further bodies lay undiscovered in a bungalow in Sheepsburn Road, Uddingston.

On 6 January 1958, the bodies of Peter Smart, his wife Doris and their eleven-year- old son Michael, were found in bed at their family home. They had been shot dead. As in previous attacks of a similar nature, the female victims clothes had been pulled up or removed to expose the body beneath. Again, it seemed that the killer had taken time out to feed himself. Curiously, the family cat had also been fed, displaying an hitherto unseen trace of tenderness in the killer. The police, under the ever watchful gaze of Detective Superintendent Alex Brown and Chief Inspector Willie Muncie, had their suspicions, indeed they pretty sure that they knew who the killer was, so it was matter of putting all the evidence together and finding that critical damning piece which would confirm the fact.

All the descriptions provided by witnesses of suspicious persons in the area close to each crime were similar, they all matched, albeit somewhat vaguely, with Peter Manuel. An entire city was in a constant state of panic, there seemed to be no motive behind the slayings, meaning that anyone living in Glasgow or surrounding district could be the next victim. The police filled the streets, officers drafted in as undercover and in uniform were keen to promote calm. Such was the saturation of police officers that criminal activity became almost impossible in certain areas, causing much unrest amongst the criminal fraternity. In Detective Inspector Tom Goodall the police had an officer with roots in the community. He had the contacts that could get vital intelligence flowing from the underworld, and knew full well that criminals would feel suffocated by the overwhelming policing levels and would to return to normaility as soon as possible. It wasn't too long before information began to come in that highlighted Manuel as number one suspect. He was despised by his own kind, information as to his bragging about being more clever than the cops and spalshing new found wealth about in bars and pubs of the city.

William Watt whose family had been murdered by the killer wasn't about to forget the matter either, since he was on a crusade to find and bring to justice the person who had destroyed his life. Through Watt's lawyer (Dowdall) a meeting between the two men took place. Manuel was in his element. He had the attenion he craved for and had information too and in some cases, information is viewed as power. Manuel couldn't resist the tempatation to guide Watt through the gruesome details of the crime, as allegedly told to him by the real killer.

The police were ready to make their move and in the early morning forced entry into the Manuel home and found Peter Manuel asleep in a bed chair. He denied murder or having any other part in such a crime, but despite his protestations he was handcuffed and taken away. With their man officially in custody the police could commit to a more thorough search of the property, recovering personal items that had clearly been removed from the home of the Smarts. There was other stolen property there too, relating to different crimes.

At Hamilton police headquarters Manuel continued to deny everything that was put to him and, quite sensationally, named another criminal: Samuel 'Dandy' McKay, as the real killer, saying that McKay had confessed and confided in him. The police at once passed the message through to McKay who retaliated accordingly. There is, they say, no honour amongst thieves. Certainly in this case no one throughout the criminal underworld had the slightest respect for Peter Manuel. Suddenly, evidence against him in relation to all kinds of crimes began to flow. William Watt came forward to tell police how he had met with Manuel who had produced from his pocket a photograph and had smugly torn it up in front of him. He recognised the photograph, it was of Anne Kneilands.

The police played another ace card when they allowed him

to see and meet with his devastated parents. His parents wanted to hear from his own lips whether he was innocent or guilty as accused. His mother looked at her nervous son in the eye and asked him to speak the truth as to what had happened. Peter Manuel broke down in tears and confessed to his sins, apologising to his parents for being such a let down to them and for getting them involved in such a situation.

A confession to killing Isabelle Cooke led to Manuel taking the police to the site in a field in Mount Vernon where they should dig. Soon they had uncovered her remains. Around her neck, tied tightly was her bra, her head scarf had been tied around her face, the knot forced into her mouth, presumably to quieten her during the attack.

Back at police headquarters Manuel compiled a written confession to the murders of Anne Kneilands, the Watt family, Margaret Brown and the Smart family. In addition to this he confessed to the murders of Isabelle Cooke and Sidney Dunn, revealing how he had caught a train to Newcastle, then took a taxi from the station and out of the city onto a country road where he shot the driver in the back of the head and slit his throat. The confession was alengthy one and provided police with every detail, including the precise location in the River Clyde where he had got rid of the murder weapons – a Webley revolver and a Beretta automatic. Both guns were recovered. He confessed to feeding the Smart family cat some tinned salmon after he had committed the murder, and to having a sleep on their couch. Police further conjectured that he returned to the Smart house several times after the murder and before the discovery of the crime, in order to feed the cat and to gloat on the result of his power over life and death. The murder of the taxi driver had occurred under English law and could not therefore be tried under the Scottish judical system, hence that matter was not tried.

Despite this, it was as comprehensive a case for the prosecution as has ever been peroduced in a court of law. A signed confession of murder is a powerful tool for the lawyer, though can also prove to be a burdon if the defence claim it was forced under duress. Therefore, the prosecution still had a great deal of work ahead of them if they were to succeed in the High Court trial in May 1958.

The drama continued in court, as Manuel sacked his entire defence team and elected to defend himself . The trial lasted for twelve whole days during which Manuel produced a great performance and extended the prosecution case to its full capacity. In his summing up to the jury Lord Cameron informed the jury that they were not there as 'avengers of blood' even though young life had been cut short in the commission of the crimes discussed. He also ruled that there should be a 'not guilty' verdict on the murder of Anne Kneilands for lack of corroboration to prove that Manuel had murdered the young woman. The jury retired at around 2.15 pm. After deliberating for two and half hours, they returned to the court at 4.46 pm. It was a unanimous verdit of guilty of seven counts of murder. Lord Cameron faced a seemingly unconcerned Peter Manuel and said: 'Peter Thomas Anthony Manuel, in respect of the verdit of guilty of capital murder and of murder done on different occasions, the sentence of the court is that you will be taken from this place to the prison of Barlinnie at Glasgow to be detained until the 19th day of June and on that day within the said prison at Glasgow and between the hours of eight and ten to suffer death by hanging.' The trial judge then adorned the black tricorn hat and added the words: 'This pronounced for doom.'

An appeal was lodged and duly rejected. Peter Manuel was executed on the morning of Friday 11 July 1958 after eating his breakfast and drinking a glass of whisky.

There has been much in the way of speculation as to how many people Peter Manuel did murder. Certainly there were many boastful comments made from within the confines of the condemned cell. It is said that he admitted to killing a further nine people in places such as Glasgow and Coventry, though his final total may be closer to eighteen such victims.

Was Manuel insane or was he simply evil? Certainly, he was lucid enough to fear the gallows, as it filled him with horror, so much so that he tried to escape the punishment of the noose by swallowing disinfectant, in what was to be a failed attempt at suicide. In my opinion that gives him an awareness of the fate that awaited him, it puts him in control of his actions and proves him to continue to display his devious cunning to the very end. Peter Manuel was evil.

CHAPTER 16

Dance With the Devil: 'Bible John'

1968

There are those who say that the city of Glasgow cannot sleep contentedly whilst one of the most notorious killers ever to have walked its streets is still on the loose. The case of 'Bible John' has provided no closure for any of the victims' families nor for those old enough to remember it. The spectre of Bible John remains in every dark street and alley and his nightmarish activities have become synonymous with the legendary Barrowlands ballroom. Bible John is very much part of Glasgow folklore, though sadly he is not a myth, but a devastatingly real nemesis from the 1960s. Each time a sexual attack on a woman within Scotland is reported in the media, associations with Bible John are cast.

At around 7.30 am on Friday 23 February 1968, sixty-seven-year-old Maurice Goodman, a joiner, of 27 Carmichael Place, Battlefield, left his home to walk through to his garage which was in the service road of Carmichael Lane, a narrow, partially cobbled lane which serves the terraced homes of Carmichael Place and Braemar Street. It was a journey Maurice carried out routinely at about the same time each day. He turned the corner into the lane and made towards his lock-up garage. Upon reaching the recess of the garage door he saw, lying on its back, with its head turned to the right, a naked body with no signs of clothing nearby. He at once reported the grisly sight to the police. By 8.10 am, Detective Sergeant Andrew Johnstone and Detective Constable Norman MacDonald arrived at the scene, called there by the two traffic officers who had been first to respond to the call. Traffic wanted nothing to do with a murder and protected the scene until the arrival of the experts. The body was confirmed as being female. None of the victim's clothing could be found near the scene, other than a pair of tan/brown sling-back shoes, and a used sanitary towel right next to the body. There were also the tell-tale signs of physical violence, on the neck, face and body, grazes and cuts and skin discoloration marks.

The investigation was taken over by Detective Superintendent Elphinstone Dalglish and, in an effort to identify the unfortunate woman, a mobile police caravan was placed at the Ledard Road end of the lane as a base for communication. Dr James Imrie, the police surgeon, carried out a cursory examination of the body at the scene and identified the probable cause of death as manual strangulation, there being ligature marks around the neck.

News of the finding of a body spread through the region like wild fire, and soon a gathering of local people had congregated at both of ends of the heavily policed Carmichael Place. Journalists too descended upon the area and began to make their own house-to-house enquiries (in some instance pre-empting the police investigation) as they desperately sought out any snippets of information for a good news story. Nobody, it seemed, knew anything. The body in the lane was a complete mystery.

Two nurses from the nearby Victoria Infirmary were brought to the lane in order to view the body as there was an assumption that the remains could be either a wandering patient or a local hospital worker, but neither of them was able to identify the remains. With no further forensic evidence available at the scene, the remains were removed around lunchtime. Within a few hours it was confirmed by post-mortem examination carried out by Professor Gilbert Forbes and Dr James Imrie that the woman had died as a result of strangulation and had been raped, beaten and violently kicked about the body prior to death. The used and discarded sanitary towel was confirmed as belonging to the victim.

There was something of a breakthrough when detectives carrying out house-to-house enquiries found someone who said: 'I heard a woman shout out, twice in quick succession "Let me go!" it was brief and I never heard it again. I thought

Pat Docker.

nothing of it at the time. It was not followed by any kind of screams or any sort of commotion really. I could not honestly say whether the woman was in distress or not, due to it all happening so quickly.'

That same evening, the *Glasgow Evening Times* ran the headline: 'MURDER IN CITY LANE – GIRL BELIEVED NUDE...AND STRANGLED'. The story provided in print the first police description of the as yet unidentified dead woman: she was of medium height, had short, dark brown wavy hair, hazel eyes, a snub nose...and wore a wedding ring on the third finger of her right hand. John Wilson, aged sixty-three, of Langside Place, a couple of hundred yards from where the body was found, sat down to read the evening papers and read of the gruesome discovery close to the home he shared with his wife Pauline, daughter Patricia and her four-year-old son Sandy. Patricia had gone out the evening before and had not yet returned home, which had somewhat concerned him as it was unusual. He wandered down to the Ledard Road police caravan and told officers that his daughter had not returned from an evening's dancing the night before. He was taken to view the body and identified it as his only

Scene at the Pat Docker murder.

child and daughter, twenty-five-year-old Patricia Wilson or Docker.

Pat Docker had worked as an auxiliary nurse at Mearnskirk Hospital, usually working the nightshift from 10.00 pm to 8.00 am, Tuesdays and Thursdays being her days off. A keen dancer, on the evening in question, it was believed that Patricia had gone to the Majestic Ballroom in Hope Street (with friends from the hospital where she worked), having left home mid-evening, wearing a yellow woollen dress, a grey duffle coat with a blue fur collar, and brown shoes; she had also been carrying a brown handbag and on her right hand was a wedding ring, which at one time had belonged to her grandmother. Family were ruled out as suspects and there was no obvious clues as to why she should be so brutally attacked and killed.

Clearly, there were a number of issues relating to the case, for instance, how she had been found naked in the lane with no sign of her clothing yet being discovered and had she been murdered in the lane or simply dumped there? Police divers carried out a search of a one-mile stretch of the nearby White Cart river, and later revealed that they had made a 'notable find', but initially refrained from stating what this was in an attempt to unnerve the killer into believing it had a 'definite bearing' on the case. This proved to be the dead woman's bracelet, part of a watchcase and the missing handbag.

Further public appeals were made by the police, providing a more detailed description of Pat's clothing on the night/ morning of her murder, clothing which was now missing. It was asked that anyone finding anything of the sort to report it to the police immediately. Further appeals to the public were made, including a request for the driver of a Morris 1000 Traveller which had been seen at about 11.10 pm on the Friday night in Langside Avenue. In a separate appeal, the police wanted to trace the driver of a white Ford Consul (375 model) seen in Braemar Street and turning into Overdale Street. A man and a woman were in the car, which drove up Overdale Street, turning into Carmichael Place. Within forty-eight hours, the two occupants of the Ford Consul were found and provided a suitable explanation for their actions, and eliminated from enquiries. A renewed appeal for the driver of the Morris 1000 Traveller to come forward was made two days later; no one ever confessed to being the driver of the said vehicle and it has never been traced. Finally, to cover all options, the police asked for any taxi driver who may have dropped a fare near the murder scene between 10.30 pm on Thursday night and 1.15am on Friday morning to come forward.

Dancers who attended the 'over 25' night at the Majestic on the night of 22 February 1968 were spoken to with a blown up photograph of Patricia being shown on a screen, accompanied by a police spokesman asking for assistance in catching the killer. Incredibly successful (fewer than twenty people remained untraced), the information completely altered the direction of the investigation. It transpired that Patricia had moved on from the Majestic ballroom and had gone to the Barrowlands ballroom for a carnival dance, which finished at midnight.

Interest in the case reached an all time high when a national newspaper distributed more than a thousand specially printed posters around the city, as well as to retail outlets. The poster displayed a recent picture of Patricia Docker and asked anyone who saw her on the murder night to come forward and telephone the police. Despite this, no valuable evidence was forthcoming and the murder of Patricia Docker was destined

Mima McDonald – murder victim.

to remain unsolved. The memory of the shocking murder in Langside soon faded from memory and the Glasgow nighttime economy continued to flourish, especially the dancing.

Jemima McDonald was a thirty-two-year old single mum, 5′ 7″ tall, of slim build, with dyed dark shoulder-length hair, showing fair roots; she lived at 15 Mackeith Street Bridgeton, not too far from the Barrowlands ballroom in the East End of Glasgow. On Saturday 16 August 1969 'Mima' was going to the dancing at the Barrowlands. She dressed, putting on her black pinafore, white frilly blouse and her cream sling-back high- heel shoes, and a brown woollen coat. Her hair, still in rollers, was covered with a brown scarf, and she was carrying a black patent leather handbag which contained her brown purse. Her older sister Margaret was looking after her three children, a common enough arrangement; so when Mima never returned that night, Margaret was not unduly concerned. Somewhat recklessly, she had done this before.

Rumours about a body in the derelict tenement block of 23 Mackeith Street began to surface, and on the Monday morning at about 10 am Margaret decided to take a look.

Barrowlands Ballroom.

There she found the partially clothed body of her sister in a bed recess. Strangled with her own tights and punched in the face, she was partially clothed. The black handbag she had with her was missing, she too had been menstruating and had a used tampon placed on her body. Her body was just twenty yards from her own home, and it was later determined that it had been there for thirty hours.

Police appealed for witnesses to come forward, anyone who may have seen her leave the Barrowlands and walk home in the direction of Bridgeton Cross, between the hours of 12 midnight and 1.30 am on Sunday morning. Jemima's walk home would take her via Bain Street, London Road, down to Landressey Street or Main Street and then into MacKeith Street. A policewoman dressed in similar clothes to those of Mima retraced the walk home in the hope of jogging witness memory.

A number of witnesses came forward, providing a description of a man who was seen to leave the Barrowlands with Mima; he was described as being twenty-five to thirty-five years of age, 6′ to 6′ 2″ tall, of slim build with a thin, pale face and reddish short fair hair, brushed back. He was said to be wearing a good quality blue suit with hand-stitched lapels and a white shirt. By 21 August 1969 the police confirmed what was already being said on the street, that the killing of Jemima McDonald could well be linked to that of Patricia Docker eighteen months earlier. They confirmed to the media that both women had indeed visited the Barrowlands Ballroom on the night of their deaths.

Mima McDonald's handbag had not been located and one theory was that children playing may have found it and either thrown it away or taken it home.

On Tuesday 26 August 1969, an identikit picture was used and released for publication in newspapers for the first time during a Scottish murder hunt.

The Barrowlands ballroom became the focus of the police investigation, regulars were interviewed and potential suspects, gauged by their appearance in comparison to the identikit. Dozens of men were pulled in and questioned by the police, all had alibi's and were removed from the investigation. By the end of October 69 these visits had all but ceased, the police had more important matters to deal with – yet another murder.

Helen Puttock – murder victim.

In October 1969, twenty-nine-year-old Helen Puttock lived with her mother and two young children at 129 Earl Street, Scotstoun. On Thursday the 30th Helen intended going out dancing with her sister Jeannie. Her husband who was home on leave from the armed services was very disappointed by this but succumbed to Helen's demands and agreed that she could go while he stayed home and looked after the children. So it was, dressed in brown tights, green nylon knickers and blue and black under slip covered by a black sleeveless dress, with a fake ocelot fur coat and black strap shoes, and carrying a red purse, the five feet eight inches tall and brunette Helen Puttock hit the town with her sister. The two women left Earl Street shortly after 8 pm, taking the bus to Glasgow Cross where they headed straight to some of the more popular city centre pubs and then on to the Barrowland ballroom.

An evening's dancing at the Barrowland was to be enjoyed, and soon both sisters were up on the dance floor 'jiggin'. Helen had managed to attract a tall handsome looking man. Jeannie too found a permanent dance partner for the evening and politely both women engaged their companions in conversation, only to find that they were rather vague when asked about themselves. Astutely, they formed the impression that both were probably married and didn't really want to give away too much about personal circumstances. It was treated with some hilarity when both men claimed their Christian

Barrowland Ballroom II.

name to be John, a typical unimaginative pseudonym to hide their true identity, both women thought, hardly unusual on a Thursday night at the Barrowlands, as the majority of people there were either married or spoken for. Jeannie's partner was a little more open and told her that he was from the Castlemilk district.

Helen's partner though, seemed a little different; he was more sophisticated and better groomed than most of the other regular punters in the ballroom. He was polite and courteous, and even held the chair out for Jeannie and Helen when they moved to sit down or stand up, displaying chivalry and manners, which was most unusual in such an environment. Even more unusual, John provided a surname too. However, Jeannie failed to hear it properly in the raucous noise of the dance hall, but thought it sounded similar to Templeton, Sempleson or Emerson. At the time it didn't seem important. Everything about this man appeared genuine and did not arouse suspicion. The four seemed to get on reasonably well and freely chatted about the music and the band. There seemed to be no hidden agenda to either man which made the evening go down that little bit better as both women relaxed.

Eventually, with the dance over, the four made to leave the hall. Jeannie wanted some cigarettes from the machine in the ballroom. It malfunctioned and, seeing she was having trouble, Helen's partner tried to help, again with no success. Assertively, he called over the manager telling him in no uncertain terms that the loss of Jeannie's money was unsatisfactory. He was calm and confident in his manner causing Jeannie to feel he was a man who was used to being obeyed, and they were given their money back.

From this point in time, John's demeanor took a turn for the worse. He seemed aggravated and told both women: 'My father says these places are dens of iniquity. They set fire to this place to get the insurance money and done it up with the money they got.' Believing it to be nothing more than a supportive off the cuff remark, which indicated his bitterness towards the management, Helen and Jeannie continued to make their way out of the hall with John. Momentarily, Jeannie turned away from Helen and John in search of her own dancing partner who had strayed away from the group. As she turned back towards her sister and her partner John something was said between the pair, which, judging by her reaction (Helen was shaking her head and smirking in disbelief), Helen did not believe. John then produced something from his jacket pocket and showed it to Helen. It was a card, probably some form of identification. Upon seeing this, Helen's attitude changed from playful disbelief to an almost stunned surprise. Whatever was upon the card had clearly now clarified to Helen that John was authentic. The four, along with other revellers, made their way from the Barrowland along Gallowgate towards Glasgow Cross. At London Road, close to Moir Street, Jeannie's partner ended his part in the group's evening by bidding them goodnight, explaining to them that he was going to catch his bus home from George Square to Castlemilk. This left the two women and the remaining man, John, to take a taxi to Scotstoun.

Helen, Jeannie and John got into a cab and made the twenty minute journey to Scotstoun, during which John became more broody and aloof. Jeannie believed that he saw her as an obstacle between himself and Helen and didn't really want her with them.

In an attempt to make the journey as pleasant as possible the women asked John about himself and what he did in the summer. He explained that his family had a caravan at Irvine. When asked what he did at New Year, he said that he didn't drink, but he preferred to pray. He also said that he was an agnostic and didn't believe in all that religious carry on, but he did know something from the Bible, and talked of Moses and a woman who had been stoned, or who had been standing at a well. Jeannie could not recognize it as a complete quote but believed it had Old Testament connotations.

John insisted that Jeannie be dropped off first, hence the taxi driver was directed to the roundabout at the bottom of Kelso Street where it stopped and she got out, bidding her sister, John and the driver goodnight, adding to Helen: 'I'll maybe see you next week.' Rudely, John ignored Jeannie and instructed the driver to move on. This was the last confirmed sighting of Helen Puttock alive.

Archie MacIntyre of 95 Earl Street, a road worker, took his black Labrador 'Smokey' down the back stairs of 95 Earl Street. It was about 7.30 am when they walked into the back court. The dog was off the lead and ran to what Archie thought was a bundle of rags near the close-mouth at the back court, when he saw it was a woman. In a panic he ran to call an ambulance as he had no idea whether she was still alive. On their arrival, the body was ice cold, and rigor mortis had taken hold.

Round the dead woman's neck was one of her own stockings with which she had clearly been strangled. There were abrasions to her jaw and the side of her head; her nose and mouth had been bleeding and there was further bruising to the face as if she had been struck by something or someone; and her clothing was in general disarray and torn. Caught between the ligature (the stocking) and her neck was some old withered dock leaves. Once again, the woman had been menstruating at the time of the attack. However, the sanitary towel had been removed and tucked under the woman's armpit. Once again, her handbag was missing.

A mobile police station in the form of a caravan was set up in Earl Street outside the entrance to number 95, and uniformed officers were called in to seal off access routes into the Earl Street tenement blocks; and to assist with house-to-house enquiries in the locality. Once again an evening out had ended in tragedy.

Later that same morning, Helen's husband, George, looked out of a window of 129 Earl Street and saw the activity a few hundred yards down the street. Dismayed that his wife had not returned home from her night out, he wandered down to the police caravan to ask what was happening, explaining that she had not come from the previous evening. The response he heard was to turn his world upside down and inside out: there had been a murder. The officer asked what she was wearing. George informed them and said that his wife was dead. Once again family an friends were interviewed. This time though, there were clues and a good sighting from Helen's sister.

A team of detectives visited the Barrowland Ballroom on the night of Saturday 1 November where they spoke to everyone

Bible John, artist's impression.

Inspector Joe Beattie, who investigated the Bible John murder case.

in attendance asking for any information that may assist their enquiries. Superintendent Joe Beattie knew that the only key witness available was Jeannie. As a result of this, the entire police investigation focused and relied upon her testimony and powers of description. Subsequently, many officers felt this to be the wrong course of action as it put more pressure on what was clearly a distraught witness.

Soon the killer was given a haunting pseudo-identity. Just as Jack the Ripper had in London some eighty-one years previously, the title would instill fear into an entire city if not nation for years to come. So it was that the term 'Bible John' was created on 4 November 1969 when the *Glasgow Herald* reported under the headline: 'Bible-quoting man sought by murder hunt police':

A man aged between 25–30, 5 foot 10 inches to 6 foot tall, of medium build, with light auburn reddish hair, styled short, and brushed to the right. Blue-grey eyes, nice straight teeth with one tooth on the upper right jaw overlapping the next tooth, fine features, and is generally of smart, modern appearance. Dressed in brownish, flecked single breasted suit, the jacket of which has three or four buttons and high lapels. There are no turn ups on the trousers and the suit is in a modern style. A knee length brownish coat of tweed or gabardine, a light blue shirt and a dark tie with red diagonal stripes.

He was wearing a wrist-watch with a broad leather strap of military style. He may smoke embassy tipped cigarettes. He is known to go to Barrowlands on occasions and is thought to go alone.

The man is thought to be called by the Christian name John. He may speak of being one of a family of two, his sister and himself, and of having had a strict upbringing and make references to the Bible. He is quite well spoken, probably with a Glasgow accent and does not appear to be engaged on heavy manual work.

The man may have marks on his face and hands of recent origin.

The police investigation floundered and continued to have little in the way of success. Thousands of people were spoken to and a group of undercover police officers attended the Barrowlands every Thursday and at weekends in the hope of catching the killer. They were easily recognisable by their dress and the men had regulation short back and side haircuts, as the description given of Bible John depicts him to also have. Eventually, the investigation was wound down and the whole series of killings were almost forgotten, revived every so often by enthusiastic journalists keen to find a new angle. Convicted rapists and those with a perverted manner have all been suspected of being the killer.

One could almost hear the cry of content amongst much of the Glasgow community, when in 1996 the body of a man who commited suicide was exhumed. It was said that he was a leading candidate for being the killer and had been interviewed by the police at the time. The press gleefully reported every detail of the 1996 exhumation with the story of Bible John killings being regurgitated, many believed for one last time. DNA evidence found at the scene and held by the police was produced and compared to that from the exhumed corpse, but there was no match, the man was not Bible John. Having pinned much hope on the story the press instantly dropped it, old wounds had been opened and once again there was no closure.

Pat Docker – murder victim.

During the dozen or so years that I have been actively researching this case I have come across countless of theories and potential candidates. I was contacted and taunted by a defrocked minister with the Christian name John. He was in Glasgow at the time and knew much about the crimes. At one stage I genuinely believed him to be connected in some way to the killings. However, when I met him and he began to speak of a 'freemason conspiracy', numerology and the underworld I reassessed my opinion.

However, one theory that I cannot rid myself of is that Bible John was not the work of one man. Certainly, the murder of Patricia Docker seems likely to have been a totally separate and individual crime, with the victim potentially having been killed elsewhere and her body dumped in the lane, possibly by someone in a car or perhaps she had been at a surrounding house. It is known that certain social functions were taking place in the area she lived in, so could she have been to one of these prior to her untimely death?

When one looks at the available evidence that has been released into the public domain and printed in the pages of the press it becomes clear that either the police did not have a lot to go on or they have decided to withhold data. As an ex-police officer I am occasionally granted permission to view the more historic case files, but not so in this instance. My efforts to view the case files pertaining to the Bible John crimes have thus far been rebuffed. In one instance in the mid 1990s I was told that no generic case file existed. Yet files do exist and the senior officer who spoke with me must surely have known that at the time.

My own curiosity leads me to suspect that the killer or killers had association with the police. Certainly Bible John seems to have been one step ahead of the police. Yet how, as the information being released to the press was, as we have already stated, minimal. Then there is the man who was seen with Helen Puttock. He produced a form of identity from his pocket – could this have been a warrant card, so displayed to allay suspicion? Furthermore, he spoke confidently and firmly when in a confrontational situation with the manager of the Barrowlands ballroom causing Jeannie to assume that he was man used to giving orders and of some discipline. Certainly the description of this person and that seen with Jemima McDonald match the archetypal image of a police officer and policemen as we have seen in this volume, are not always the paragons of virtue everyone would want them to be. Despite everything else, many would not be averse to going to the Barrowlands on a Thursday evening for the over 25s night.

The majority of police officers are fine upstanding citizens and I do not criticise nor underestimate the outstanding work they achieve in the communities they serve. However, I am aware that some officers of the era had their suspicions that the killer of Jemima McDonald and Helen Puttock at least, could have been the work of a policeman, perhaps not a Glasgow one, maybe an outsider who lived in the area. I was once told by a retired officer that it was his belief that two police officers were involved, one keeping watch while the other commited the crime. Could this have been the other 'John' who had been with Jeannie on the night of Helen Puttock's murder?

The case of Bible John is an intriguing one and one that will continue to throw up as many questions as it answers. Will it be solved? Yes, one day soon, I believe it will.

CHAPTER 17

Gunshots Across a City: James Griffiths

1969

Blackburn Place, Ayr, is nice place, very nice. A mere stone throw away from the Esplanade where one can take in stunning views across the Firth of Clyde, it was and remains a much sought after residential area, with wonderfully large houses reflecting the good, clean and healthy status of the district. In 1969, the peaceful tranquility of Blackburn Place was brought to a temporary close as the nation's press converged on the town and in particularly the tiny cul-de-sac situated just off the Blackburn Road.

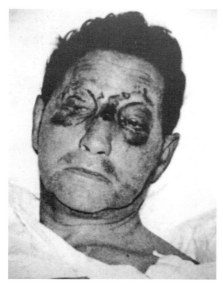

Abraham Ross.

Abraham and Rachel Ross were two very well respected members of Ayr society. Aged sixty-seven and seventy-two respectively, the couple tended to keep themselves to themselves, enjoying their peaceful lives. They resided at number 2 in the cul-de-sac, a smart home in keeping with the affluence of the immediate area. On the night of 5 July, their house became the scene of a barbaric crime that resulted in death. Asleep in their bed, Abraham Ross was awakened by the unnerving sound of intruders in their home. Banging and thudding noises were heard as furniture was shifted by the burglars. Abraham, keen to ascertain the source of the noises and to frighten them off, clambered out of bed, making plenty of noise himself, and was about to embark on a room by room search of the house in the hope that his presence would frighten off the intruders. Ordinarily, such actions would have the desired effect, however, these were no ordinary burglars.

The first thing Abraham saw was the silhouette of two people who, from the tone of their voices, he realised were both men. Within moments he was felled by one of them, using a sharp-edged weapon which knocked him clean off his feet and momentarly stunning him. In a state of absolute

Rachael Ross.

shock, Ross could do little as the two intruders bound his hands and feet with rope and nylon stockings, gagging him and preventing him crying out for help. The sickening noise of her husband being beaten must have terrified poor Rachel Ross, but once again the intruders acted swiftly. They burst into the bedroom where she lay petrified on her bed, forcibly manhandled her from it and threw her onto the floor. One of the men knelt heavily upon her chest while the other tied her with rope and more nylon stockings. Systematically, Abraham and Rachel Ross were tortured into revealing to the two men where all their valuables were kept within the house. It was a terrifying ordeal as the ageing couple could nothing to defend themselves against the cowardly attack. Eventually, the men discovered what they had come for, cash. They left the house with around £1,000 and other valuables and drove out of the close in a car.

Unable to move and thus alert the police as to the crime, it was some time before the couple were discovered. One can only imagine the torment they both went through as they lay unable to defend themselves, waiting for someone to discover them. Sadly, worse was still to come. Rachel Ross, as a result of the assault and attack, was critically ill and just three days after the event, passed away. The Glasgow police were quick to act upon their gut feeling and responded with a swift arrest. Patrick Meehan was taken into custody. Curiously, Meehan had no official record of violence, yet the police, through their sources, knew that he had been in Ayrshire on the night in question. This was a fact that the prisoner never denied. He was to suggest that he and one other person were on their way to Stranraer to case an office they were to break into. Subsequently, and one cannot speculate as to the validity of the affair, a distraught and emotional Abraham Ross identified Meehan as one of the men who broke into his home and attacked him and his wife.

Meehan's alibi rested on the man who accompanied him on his trip to Stranraer. The man was identifed as James Griffiths, a thirty-four-year-old who hailed from Rochdale in Lancashire. He too was a hardened criminal and had a record of various offences from the age of thiteen. Griffiths had at one

time shared a cell at Parkhurst prison on the Isle of Wight with Archie Hall (known as the 'monster butler') and Meehan. His criminal stock and reputation was raised substantially when he escaped from Parkhurst, getting away from the island and back onto the English mainland, before being recaptured. From that day, the men had become close friends, with a common criminal purpose. Now, however, Meehan had to call on Griffiths to do him a favour and provide his alibi; in doing so, Griffiths would essentially free both himself and Meehan of any possible charges. It was ascertained that Griffiths was hiding in a property in Holyrood Crescent, in Glasgow's West End, where he was using the alias 'Mr Douglas'.

   Griffiths himself had little or nor respect for anyone, a womaniser, he would boast about his sexual promiscuity and activities, something that often repelled his fellow inmates. He was regarded by many as small-time crook with a big ego and even greater imagination. Little could anyone know or realise that inside, he was a man who hated himself, a simmering pot of anger with a real hatred for figures of authority. He deeply disliked incarceration, saw it as the authorities getting one over on him, the same establishments who he believed were collectively thick and incompetent, not shrewd, clever and cunning like himself. He felt anger every moment of his waking day, for the affluent society and what they represented, filling him with contempt. This would temporarily dissipate when he criminally relieved the well-off of parts of their amassed fortunes. Mentally, Griffithss was a psychological wreck, a walking time bomb, a disaster waiting to happen.

Early in the morning of 15 July 1969, two detectives visited the suspected hideout and property where James Griffiths was believed to be residing. Before visiting him there was a need to confirm that 'Mr Douglas' lived there, hence the officers first spoke with the caretaker of the flats. The information was confirmed and the police left the building without visiting the watchful Griffiths who had been watching from an upstairs window and recognised the two visitors as plain clothed bogeys. He was surprised when they left the building.

It was about 10.30 am that same day when the police returned to 14 Holyrood Crescent which was situated on the bend of the road, offering ideal views in both directions for the occupant of the attic flat. Five detectives including member of the Regional Crime Squad approached the door of Douglas' flat and made an enquiring knock. A burst of gunfire from from within the flat ensued, targeted at the unarmed police officers gathered outside the front door. One officer, Detective Constable William Walker, fell to ground, struck by one of the randomly fired bullets. The police retreated with haste, assisting the injured officer down the stairs and out onto the street below. The officers had barely set foot on the pavement outside when further indiscriminate shooting commenced, innocent passers by running for cover and hiding behind cars as the bullets flew. One wholly innocent man, Robert McAdam, was struck in the leg by a bullet in nearby Barrington Drive and, a few seconds later, another man, John Currie, was shot and injured while making his way along Napiershall Street. The entire area was in a state of pandemonium. For a few minutes the gunfire ceased, only for the gunman to emerge from the premises, run to a parked car in Great Western Road, open the boot and remove a belt of cartridges before resuming his shooting spree. In the few seconds he was out on the street, the gunman fired off several rounds, wounding another four innocent victims: Samuel Collins (thigh wound), Jack Kerr (arm wound), Ian Wilson (neck wound) and Mary McKinnon (shoulder and side wound). He then disappeared back into the flat. Back-up police patrols arrived, and the entire area was sealed off. Armed police arrived too and took up strategic positions to allow them the best opportunity of getting a shot at the gunman. There they waited for the next order to come from the officer in command, Detective Chief Superintendent Tom Goodall. The wait continued...

The gunman, meanwhile, had absconded the scene, leaving the property via the back garden and clambering over a high wall to drop down into Landsdowne Crescent Lane. Unsure of where to turn next, he moved through Herbert Street and out along North Woodside Road towards the River Kelvin. As he approached the bridge crossing the river he saw a number of people pointing at him and shouting out messages, presumably to nearby police. Without a care for their safety he fired off several rounds at the group before running off toward Garriochmill Road, but fortunately no one was physically injured in this volley of shots. The police meanwhile had been alerted by members of the public as to the gunman's location and were quickly in pursuit. The chase was on.

In desperation, the gunman saw a man leaving the *Grapes Bar* and get into his car in nearby Henderson Street. Approaching the car, the gunman fired off a single round into the driver, Mr Kerr, then swung open the car door and pulled the wounded driver from the vehicle, and drove off, leaving the injured man clutching at the bullet wound in his arm. Mobilised police offciers were quickly on the scene. In one vehicle was Detective Superintendent Binnie and Detective Superintendent Finlayson. Binnie got a good look at the gunman who was now driving a stolen car and immediately recognised him as James Griffiths. The vehicle registration number was circulated on the police airwaves with a stark warning to any officer who saw it not to approach the driver, who was armed and extremely dangerous, but to simply make note of the route.

By now Griffiths was extremely agitated and was fast losing the ability to think rationally and, in panic, crashed the stolen car near the Round Toll. Escaping from the vehicle, he ran into the *Round Toll Bar* in Possil Road and slammed the door shut behind him. The custodians of the bar, James and Jean Connolly, were mortified to see the angry man enter their premises and produce two revolvers, pointing them at customers and staff with the threat to shoot and kill anyone who moved. In some ridiculous and totally unnecessary act of bravado he fired a shot at sixty-five-year-old Billy Hughes, a customer who offered no physical or other threat to him. Hughes was to later die as a result of the injury sustained. No one dared move as Griffiths walked up to the bar and demanded a drink, snatching a bottle of brandy and swigging generously from the mouth of the bottle. James Connolly was angered by the situation and seized the opportunity to take hold of the gun-brandishing Griffiths as he was drinking. Grabbing him in a bear hug, he manhandled him out of the bar and onto the pavement outside. It was a momentary respite, as Griffiths was quickly back inside and fired off a volley of bullets at no one in particular, incredibly missing everyone in the pub.

The activity around the area and the sound of gunshots soon caused an impromptu gathering of members of the public outside the bar, each of whom was cowering behind cars and buildings for safety. A lorry driver, John Craig, was flagged down by the gathered crowd and alerted as to the life threatening danger he was in. Looking up, he saw Griffiths emerge from the door of the bar and start to walk toward his lorry. Craig leapt down from the cab and hid behind a lamp-post. Griffiths fired more shots into the crowd, one at a man who lunged at him in an attempt to detain him. The brave man, Ian Shaw, fell to the floor. The other injured man, Peter Paterson, also suffered from a gun shot wound. Griffiths, unconcerned about the trail of carnage and devastation he was leaving behind, climbed into the lorry and drove off along Possil Road. With the police in distant pursuit, the lorry was being followed by a taxi-driver who had open communication with the police information room, and continued to Kay Street, a cul-de-sac off Springburn Road.

By the time the first police arrived at the scene, traffic and crowd congestion caused mayhem for other teams of officers making their way to the Springburn area. The lorry itself, was parked at the bottom of Kay Street. From a distance there was no sign of Griffiths in the cab or nearby. Cautiously, the police approached the abandoned lorry. Incredibly, in all the excitement no one had thought to clear the street and immediate area of the public, and a crowd of curious folk appear to have been allowed into Kay Street, thereby putting their lives in danger.

Within a few moments, the gunfire resumed, Griffiths shooting randomly at the crowd from an upstairs window of 26 Kay Street. A baby in a pram had been abandoned by a terified mother who had fled to safety. Stranded on the street, the child lay unharmed, as bullets whistled and ricocheted all around. A policeman on hearing the screams of the terrified mother, edged his way back to the pram, seized the child and managed to pass it to a resident and safety, through the window of ground floor flat.

Griffiths meanwhile became bored with shooting into a street that was now empty of people. Instead, he moved to the rear of the property and turned his attentions onto a children's playground in Elmvale Street, which was brimming with dozens of children and families. Griffiths let loose several rounds, directly into those in the playground. The childish screams of enjoyment turned to screams of pain and terror as eighteen-year-old Irene Reid fell to the ground, struck in the thigh by a shot fired by Griffiths; and next an eight-year-old boy, Peter Traynor, was struck by a bullet. Though not seriously injured, it was still very much a traumatic injury for such a young child. Another man was shot in the neck. Something had to be done and done quickly if the innocent lives of more victims were to be saved.

With Griffiths seemingly obsessed and focused on causing serious injury or worse to as many people as he could there was an opportunity that police could gain access into 26 Kay Street and catch him unawares when he was in the act of randomly shooting from the windows. Detective Chief Superintendent Finlayson and Detective Sergeant Smith reached the front door of the flat. The lock had been blasted away, leaving the door open and insecure, but in a shut position. Gently squeezing open the vertical letterbox of the door, Finlayson looked inside. Along the lobby he could see scattered there dozens of empty cartridge cases, then the policeman saw Griffiths. Tucked under his left arm was a shot gun, in his other hand a rifle. Like a Mexican bandit, he had two belts of live cartridges strapped around his body, one of which was slung over his shoulder and the other strapped around his waist like a belt. It was a scene more akin to the wild west of Amercia rather than Glasgow.

Finlayson whispered instructions to Smith, telling him that he would shoot at Griffiths through the open letterbox, not to kill but to disarm him. As soon as that shot had been fired both officers would rush into the flat and physically take Griffiths down and remove the firearms and ammunition from him. He desperately wanted to take Griffiths alive and see him stand trial and justice prevail. Taking aim, he looked through the letterbox only to see Griffiths staring back down the lobby towards the front door; but before the gunman could react, Finlayson fired into Griffiths' shoulder and saw him drop to the floor. The officer rushed in and disarmed the prostrate gunman. Finlayson gave the all clear to the officers outside the flat and was about to speak to Griffiths to tell him he was under arrest, when he realised that something was wrong. The gunman wasn't moving or breathing. He was dead. Distraught, the officer looked at the wound in the killer's shoulder, and could not understand how that shot could have killed him.

It later transpired that the bullet had ricocheted from a bone in Griffiths' shoulder, round his rib cage and into his heart. His actions in killing the man was something Finlayson was never to forget, even though he had done so accidentally and by a freak situation, it was a heavy burdon for a man of such high principle to carry. Meanwhile, with James Griffiths now dead, Patrick Meehan's alibi had disappeared, resulting in him being tried for the murder of Rachel Ross and found guilty. Meehan continued to plead his innocence from within prison and eventually secured a royal pardon in 1976, after having served seven years for a crime he did not commit. The despised gunman, James Griffiths, was formally disowned by family and associates who found his actions both repulsive and unforgivable. He was given a pauper's funeral and today lies in an unamrked grave in Linn Cemetery, Glasgow. As for the identity of the killers of Rachel Ross, one man has confessed to the crime to a secretly-filmed television crew, but he later retracted the admission. He provided an insight into the layout of the house at 2 Blackburn Place that only someone who had been inside could have known.

The gallantry of the civilians during the quest to bring James Griffiths into custody saw the Corporation Medal for Bravery awarded to three members of the public: an ambulance man who endagnered his own life to save others, John Preston; James Connolly, the manager of the *Round Toll Bar* who had tried to restrain a gun-wielding Griffiths; and also to Ian Shaw, who had also tried to stop Griffiths in Possil Road.

As a sad associated issue to this vicious crime, just three months after the Griffiths shoot out, Detective Chief Superintendent Tom Goodall, Head of the Criminal Investigation Department since July 1963, suddenly died of a heart attack, suffered on 12 October 1969. Goodall remains of the finest officers to ever serve in and lead the force. The ever increasing pressure of solving crimes that were becoming more and more dangeorus and reckless caused him to be another victim. Goodall worked relentlessly to clear the street of Glasgow criminals and to keep them safe. He should be recognised and recalled as a fine ambassador and an achiever in his goals.

CHAPTER 18

Double Cop Killing: Howard Wilson

1969

Howard Charles John Wilson was an everyday nobody, a man with big ideas that were clearly beyond his status and academic grasp. Born to middle class parents, Wilson was educated at Glasgow Academy and, like thousands of others, attained his Higher Leaving Certificate. It is known that Wilson did not stand out amongst his peers, an average student who at times could be easily led by those people in whose presence his own insecurities took over and caused him to act in a subservient manner, running errands and doing the dirty work for the confident sort he so admired and desperately wanted to be like. Despite this, he never found himself in any serious trouble at the Academy, and in the main was reasonably well liked, though one suspects that this was primarily by those of a similar sort and because these people admired him because of his abilities as an athlete, an activity in which he did excel.

On leaving school Wilson carried out the statutory two years' National Service he was required to, which provided him with new found confidence. His weak and often submissive manner disappeared once he donned the uniform which he believed provided him with respect and authority. The discipline instilled in the services met with his liking as it meant that everyone was treated in the same manner and had to live by the same body of rules. Here at least no one could see him for the weak man that he undoubtedly was. On completion of his National Service, Wilson applied for and was successfully accepted in the City of Glasgow Police. How fortunate he must have felt, the police service provided him with the ideal cover to disguise his insecurities: a smart uniform. Now he could truly be the arrogant bully he had yearned to be for much of his life.

Wilson was generally regarded by his fellows as an uninspiring police officer, though he did received nine commendations for his zeal and must have been somewhat effective as a uniformed officer, it is said that he would pursue a fleeing absconder from the scene of a crime, through the streets of Glasgow for many miles until they were captured, and in a far more effective manner than any motor vehicle could pursue. Hence the commendations for his zeal. Many of his colleagues progressed into fields of specialism such as the CID. That of course would not have wholly suited Wilson who effectively hid behind the uniform. An attempt to achieve promotion failed miserably as the successful passing of sergeant exams was beyond him. He took this as a personal insult and blamed the force as opposed to his own failings.

Desperate for more money, Wilson looked at other, easier alternatives to achieve greater financial reward. His attitude towards a life in the cops changed dramatically as the realisation that he didn't have the brain to achieve the promotion and attention he felt he deserved. By the latter end of the 1960s, he had resolved to leave the force as soon as possible, probably desperate to show the police up for what *he* believed they were: a body of brainwashed clones incapable of thinking for themselves and easily outsmarted by the criminal. He wanted to achieve greater things and so resigned from the force, taking out a bank loan and opened up a greengrocer's business which he called 'The Orchard'. He recruited a junior partner, twenty-one-year-old Archibald McGleachy who possessed experience, albeit somewhat limited, as a greengrocer. The young man was heavily under the influence of his business partner and employer, Howard Wilson. Ultimately, the business venture had been ill thought through and was a resounding flop. Within several month's Wilson was losing so much money that bankruptcy seemed the only option available to him. He had a wife and two young children to provide for, he was failing them, the rent on his shop premises was gradually building up as payments were missed. Once this downward spiral had commenced, Wilson's old insecurities quickly surfaced. He openly blamed the police for his situation, claiming that had they been astute enough to have given him his promotion then he would not be in the desperate straits he now found himself. It was such thought of the police that first provided him with an effective solution to his money worries. In his mind the authorities were so blind to the ways of the clever criminal that such a person could commit crimes for many years without ever being detected.

They say that birds of a feather flock together, that was certainly the case with Howard Wilson who orchestrated a meeting with and managed to recruit the services of two other ex-policemen, John Sim and Ian Donaldson, both of whom had their own 'issues' with the force. Together, with Wilson acting as lead, the trio plotted a bank robbery and enrolled Archie McGleachy as their getaway driver.

At 3.27 pm, on 16 July 1969 the British Linen Bank in Williamswood, Renfrewshire was about to close for business for the day when four men, dressed in smart pin-striped suits, bowler hats and each carrying a briefcase entered the establishment. One counter clerk was to describe the men as having the look of 'auditors' about them. Strangely, the men stood furtively in a group and didn't immediately approach the counter staff. Instead, they waited until the last customer had been served. Within seconds, the men pulled stocking masks from their pockets, slipped them over their heads in an attempt to disguise their features and calmly walked up to the counter producing firearms and pointing them at the shocked and terrified clerks

The men then tied and gagged the four members of the bank staff and bundled them into the manager's office, additionally advising them that if no one does anything silly then no one will get hurt. With this achieved, the manager, who was the only one not to be bound and gagged, was instructed to open the safe. The masked intruders continued to fill their briefcases with cash removing a total of £25,306 and then, with incredible arrogance, walked from the premises, closing the bank entrance door behind them as they did so. The robbery team were not as composed as they would have their hostages believe and although they got away with a total of £20,876, they left behind a briefcase that contained £4,430. By the time the alarm was raised, Wilson and his team was long gone and with bank staff unable to provide adequate facial descriptions, their seemed little chance of the crime being detected. The media were quick to latch onto the details of the crime and at least one newspaper referred to it as the 'City Gent Robbery.'

The success of the raid made the gang all the more greedy as Wilson was full of himself and fancied his luck at further outsmarting the cops with another bank raid. The rest of the gang, not being the smartest bunch in the world, had quickly squandered their takings of the proceeds and needed more. Every one of them, with the exception of young Archie McGleachy, fancied their chances. The young man was a little more aware of the potential dangers a second bank robbery risked. He opted out and said he would have nothing more to do with the gang. He was given a sweetener payment of £1000, effectively buying his silence. In somewhat mysterious circumstances, he completely disappeared in the summer of 1969. A police search revealed no sightings or leads as to what had happened to him. To this day he is still missing. There remains speculation that he was killed by the gang and his remains dumped in the foundations of the Kingston Bridge in Glasgow.

The gang of four had now become a gang of three and remained focused on another bank robbery. On 29 December 1969 one of the gang members paid a visit to the Clydesdale Bank in Bridge Street, Linwood, Renfrewshire and quizzed a clerk as to the intricacies of opening a new account relating to a plant hire business. The unsuspecting clerk provided all the relevant information and the gang member left with the promise that he would return the following day with two of his friends.

It was 3.15 pm, on 30 December 1969 when the raiders brazenly struck once again. This time, without masks or cover, they marched into the bank and asked to see the manager regarding an account. The manager, wasn't there, but his assistant took the three men through to his office, totally unaware that the branch was about to be robbed. Once inside, the gang brandished a hand gun that was pressed to the assistant's temple, and the other two men produced a dagger and a knife. They also carried a number of pillowcases, some string and a number of suitcases. A pillowcase was flung over his head and his hands tightly bound.

The robbers came out of the back office and to the front counter, and four unfortunate customers in the bank at the time were held at gunpoint. The safe was opened and the cases filled with cash. Another staff member, with a knife held to his throat, was forced to open his cash drawer, which contained silver coins. These were also removed. In total the gang got away with less of a haul, yet it was still a substantial £14,212. The getaway vehicle was driven back to Glasgow at high speed and pulled into its destination in Niddrie Street. There the gang had a carried their haul into a tenement close in Allison Street, it took them two trips to clear the boot and get everything into the house. Quite amazingly, two minutes away from where the gang was holed up was the headquarters of Glasgow police's Southern Division, an incredible display of the contempt Wilson had for his ex-employers. He truly believed that he was a far superior being in every way. By chance, Inspector Andrew Hyslop and Constable Sellars were stuck in the Allison Street traffic whilst in a panda car. The Inspector noticed the gang of three carrying heavy suitcases into the close and recognised two of them as ex-police officers, Howard Wilson and John Sim. Hyslop was a copper's copper, straight and with an integrity that caused everyone who knew him to hold him in the highest regard. Gut instinct told the Inspector that something was wrong. Informing his driver to pull over and park up, he called for back up as he wanted to go into the house to check out the contents of the suitcase the men had laboured with.

A few minutes later, Detective Constables Edward Campbell, Angus McKenzie and Edward Barnett arrived at the scene, and soon the five officers were knocking on the door of 51 Allison Street.

Howard Wilson answered the door, acknowledging his recognition of the officers, he invited them into the house. Hyslop wasn't about to partake in social niceties, he told

Tenement building where Wilson killed two policemen.

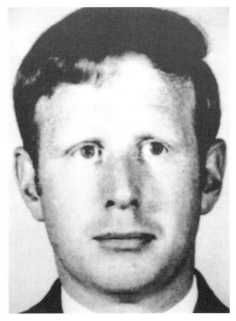

Detective Angus McKenzie, killed by Howard Wilson.

Wilson that he wanted to know what was in the suitcases they had brought into the house a few minutes earlier. Wilson played innocent and wounded, claiming that he couldn't believe his old friends would treat him or suspect him of anything suspicious. A few minutes later, a sack bearing the logo of the Clydesdale Bank and stuffed with bank notes was found. One of the criminals managed to sneak out of the house without being seen, leaving Wilson and Sim to face his ex-colleagues and take the rap. Hyslop moved from room to room searching for all the property he had seen the men with, when suddenly Howard Wilson produced a firearm and pointed it straight at the Inspector's head. He pulled the trigger, there was a misfire, then he pulled it again and blew off half of Andrew Hyslop's face. Incredibly, the wounded policeman was still conscious but unable to move a muscle.

On hearing the shot, the remaining police officers charged into the room where Hyslop and Wilson were. Angus McKenzie was first, he was shot through the head and fell to the floor, seriously wounded. Edward Barnett stood no chance as he came round the corner and met full on with another bullet fired by Wilson, again to the head. At this point, the prostrate and badly wounded McKenzie made a groaning noise. Wilson walked over to him and looking down upon the face of a man who he knew and had served beside, he fired another shot into his brain, killing him outright.

Constable Sellars, unable to make his escape, locked himself in the bathroom and was frantically calling on his police radio for urgent back up.

Howard Wilson was like a man possessed, he despised the fact that the police had out-manoeuvred him, even if it was by pure chance. He had no options available to him, all the officers now had to die. He kicked down the bathroom that acted as a barrier between himself and Constable John Sellars sufficiently to get his hand and the gun inside. However, Sellars was not about to go down without a fight and he kicked and pushed against the door preventing his assailant entry. Inspector Hyslop meanwhile had tried to speak out. Wilson walked over to him and placed the gun to the officer's head. He pulled the trigger, but nothing happened. Detective

Detective Edward Barnett, killed by Howard Wilson.

Constable Campbell seized the opportunity to rush the gunman and managed to disarm him and place him under arrest. This despite Wilson screaming at his partner in crime John Sim to help him. Sim stood in silence, knowing that Wilson had gone too far, he wanted no part in murder and submissively awaited his own arrest. The third robber, who had fled the house was arrested a few hours later at his home address. He put up no fight.

Constable Barnett later died of his injuries, whereas Inspector Hyslop survived his awful attack and returned to duty for a brief time, though the horrors of event were never to leave his waking mind. Undoubtedly, a true and genuine hero.

At the subsequent trial Wilson was found guilty of murder and robbery and sentenced to a minimum of twenty-five years for the double murder and a further twelve years for the robbery. The other two gang members and ex-policemen were each sentenced to twelve years imprisonment. None of the gang confessed to the murder or claimed to know the whereabouts of missing Archie McGleachy.

There were public calls for the policeman killer to be executed. Ultimately, these fell on politically deaf ears. Indeed,

Howard Wilson being led away to prison.

Weapons used to murder two police officers.

Howard Wilson on release from prison.

rather than commit Wilson to the tortuous life his actions thoroughly deserved, in 1994 he was reclassified as a category D prisoner, giving him privileges, one of which would be three days a week work release. Police officers from across the United Kingdom were outraged by the decision. A more recent photograph of Howard Wilson shows him with a full beard. It's a well used belief within the police service that anyone wearing a beard is hiding behind it. Never can a more accurate assumption be as relevant to any man. The cowardly and insipid looking Howard Wilson is undoubtedly an insecure and untrustworthy person who deserves no sympathy and no second chance.

Index